A Quaker Ecology:

Meditations on the Future of Friends

by Cherice Bock

A Quaker Ecology

Meditations on the Future of Friends

Barclay Press, Inc.
Newberg, Oregon
www.barclaypress.com

Cover photo and author photo by Joel Bock

Printed in the United States of America.

ISBN 978-1-59498-034-3

The content of this manuscript was originally delivered as the Bible Half-Hours at the annual sessions of New England Yearly Meeting, August 1–9, 2020. I offer my deep gratitude to those who served as my elders: from New England Yearly Meeting, Mary Hopkins and Jean Rosenburg; and from Sierra-Cascades Yearly Meeting of Friends, Dove John.

Abstract/Summary:

In our best moments, Friends have been in the middle of the action around the social justice issues of each time period, discerning to the best of their abilities the direction the Inward Light leads and speaking truth to power. In our own time, climate justice can no longer be ignored if we want to have a healthy planet to live on and if we want to participate in the heart of the justice movements of the twenty-first century.

To work on climate justice requires Quakers in the United States to revisit the practices and history of the Religious Society of Friends, recognizing the ways we have been complicit in unjust land acquisition, natural resource depletion, the intersecting injustices surrounding environmental racism, classism, and gender disparities, and the impacts of globalization. This book offers a series of meditations on the Quaker ecology, both internally in our denomination as well as in our connections to the world around us. It forms an invitation to participate in an Eco-Reformation, altering the trajectory of our Society through re-membering our history and reimagining our future as participants in the community of all life.

Table of Contents

About the Author:

Cherice Bock is a recorded Quaker minister and a member of North Valley Friends in Oregon. She served as one of the founding co-clerks of Sierra-Cascades Yearly Meeting of Friends from 2017 to 2020. Bock holds a master of divinity degree from Princeton Theological Seminary and a master of science in environmental studies from Antioch University New England, and she is a Ph.D. candidate in the same field. She teaches at the college and seminary level in the areas of Bible, theology, and environmental justice, and she works as the creation justice advocate at Ecumenical Ministries of Oregon. She edits Barclay Press's Friends Bible study curriculum, *Illuminate*.

The current volume originated in Bock's Bible Half-Hour sessions at New England Yearly Meeting in 2020, and she also presented on the topic of Quakers and creation care as a scholar in residence at Berkeley Friends Church's Quaker Heritage Day (2018) and Reedwood Friends Church's Center for Christian Studies (2017). With Stephen Potthoff, Bock co-edited the book *Quakers, Creation Care, and Sustainability*, volume 6 in the Friends Association for Higher Education series Quakers and the Disciplines. Her other writings, publications, and media can be accessed at http://chericebock. com.

1. Twenty-First Century Quaker Faithfulness: An Eco-Reformation

The year 2020 is one we will look back on as a year of intense and rapid social change. It was the strangest, most disappointing, and, in some ways, most exciting year of my life so far. When I delivered this message in late July and early August of 2020, I was experiencing pain and fear over the pandemic and its various impacts. Along with much of the rest of the nation and world, I experienced anger and grief about the murders of George Floyd, Ahmaud Arbery, Breonna Taylor, and so many other Black Americans who have lost their lives due to police brutality. At the same time, 2020 was a year of incredible hope and energy in the movements for Black lives and the protests, particularly the ones near me in and around Portland, Oregon. It has been eye-opening and invigorating to try to figure out how to be part of this movement in true solidarity. I will share more on this topic in section 4.

In June 2020, I felt worried about what I could say to New England Yearly Meeting because we were in the midst of so much social and economic turbulence, and it all felt so heavy. What message could I bring that could speak to the gravity of that moment but that also would not bring on more of a burden? For a while in the spring, it felt like we were all sprinting to get through the pandemic shut-downs and the early protests. How could I speak a message into that exhaustion, I wondered. In the couple of weeks before yearly meeting, although nothing really improved, I felt our country shifting into more of a marathon mode. We were still exhausted, but we were in it for the long haul, realizing the destination may be farther away than we had thought. We were at a point where we recognized we had gone through a significant enough change that we could not just go back to normal: a shift needed to happen. In some ways, it was a scary moment. We could tip into a really horrific phase. That danger felt particularly real in 2020. But we continue to be in a time period that holds a unique opportunity for positive change. That possibility for positive change will form the focus for this booklet.

This introductory section contains four parts:

1. queries to set the stage about ourselves as Friends;
2. introductory stories about myself, so you get a sense of who I am;
3. engaging with a passage from the Bible; and
4. describing the concept of an Eco-Reformation and some other important definitions that will set the stage for the rest of the booklet.

First, a query: Why are you a Quaker?[1] Why did you become a Quaker, and what makes you continue to be one? Reflect on that for a moment in your heart.

Readers may not know me well, but Quakerism is a deep part of my heritage and identity. I'm a convinced Friend as well as a birthright one, and I care deeply and intensely about our global Quaker family.

---

1   This message was delivered to a Quaker audience. If you are a member of a different tradition or no particular faith, I welcome you into this conversation about the interaction between tradition and current context. You can ask a similar question about your own faith tradition, or about your choice to not participate in a faith tradition.

Yet behind my question is a deeper query: Does Quakerism need to continue? I don't ask this question to make you defensive, but in all honesty, I want us to ask ourselves this question as a denomination. Does Quakerism need to continue? If the answer is yes, then what is our particular work today as Friends in the midst of a global community? What is our work in this moment of transition, of social and political unrest and opportunity?

I offer this query as a love letter to my broad Quaker family. I also ask this to New England Yearly Meeting (NEYM) because from what I know of you, you're about as close to what I would hope Quakers would be doing as any body of Friends, and so I have a reasonable hope that you can take what I have to say as a challenge to keep doing the work you are doing and intensify it. I was encouraged to hear and read about Lisa Graustein's plenary last year[2] and the minutes she referred to regarding NEYM's repudiation of the Doctrine of Discovery,[3] statements against racism and other aspects of injustice,[4] and NEYM's commitment to reduce greenhouse gas emissions by 10 percent in 2018–2019 and another 10 percent in 2019–2020.[5] You're engaging in hard

---

2   Lisa Graustein, virtual plenary sessions, New England
    Yearly Meeting 2019, https://neym.org/recordings/news/
    invitation-2019-annual-sessions-plenary.
3   "Minute Repudiating the Doctrine of Discovery," New
    England Yearly Meeting Minutes 2013, Minute 2013–52,
    https://neym.org/minute-repudiating-doctrine-discovery.
4   For example, "A Time for Repentance and Transformation,"
    New England Yearly Meeting, June 5, 2020, https://neym.org/
    news/2020/06/time-repentance-and-transformation.
5   New England Yearly Meeting Minutes 2018, Minute
    2018–36.

conversations, making changes, sticking together as a community, and actively standing up for justice.

Does Quakerism need to continue? The catalyst for our denomination's beginning was George Fox's experience of Christ personally and immediately, and he found others who had a similar experience.[6] Dr. Amanda Kemp offered a plenary session to the NEYM community. After hearing her share, I wonder if the reason we often go back to this story of Fox as our beginning point is because it was a moment before any trauma in our denomination, it was a moment where we can each feel and resonate with his "breaking open to be the unfathomable being he could be," as Amanda put it.[7] From this moment, when he was broken open and connected with the Unity of the Divine Life, a movement emerged. The early Friends made the polite company of their day uncomfortable, and they themselves experienced great discomfort: beatings, jail time in deplorable conditions, and persecution in a multitude of forms. They were not perfect by any means, and I'm not saying we should emulate them in all things. But why were they willing to experience such discomfort and persecution? Because they experienced the Spirit so intensely and created a community bound together in such love and support that they felt the courage to enact the kin-dom of God[8] to the best of their understanding.

---

6 George Fox, *The Journal of George Fox*, ed. John L. Nickalls (Philadelphia: Cambridge University Press, 1997).

7 Amanda Kemp, plenary session, New England Yearly Meeting annual sessions, August 2, 2020, https://youtu.be/tC_LGjUaT3w.

8 Ada María Isasi-Díaz, "Defining Our 'Proyecto Histórico': 'Mujerista' Strategies for Liberation," *Journal of Feminist Studies in Religion*, 9, no. 1/2 (Spring–Fall, 1993): 17–28.

What about us? Will we have that kind of courage, and will we be that kind of community for each other? Can this happen within the bounds of what we know as Quakerism, or do we need to break open so much that it will feel like starting over?

Can you feel how this moment in history is pregnant with the intensity of spiritual power (and cultural unrest) that we look back on in the lives of the first generation of Friends? Take a moment and tap into that spiritual power. Can you feel it across the miles (and now, across time)? I was hopeful as I typed this, and I am hopeful now that we are experiencing that same Presence, the Light and Love who gathers us all, "as in a net,"[9] into a spiritual community ready for radical and Spirit-filled action. I hope and pray that we are a generation who can listen and respond, who can participate in the renewal of creation that the community of all life so desperately needs right now.

And so, with hopefully equal parts humility and conviction, I offer you this series of Bible Half-Hours, which I have titled "A Quaker Ecology: Meditations on the Future of Friends." Amanda Kemp brought up Proverbs 27:18 in her plenary session, "Without vision, the people perish," and I'm offering to you, with open hands, my piece of the puzzle as we envision and discern together about the future of our small but mighty denomination.

My main point this week is that for Friends in the United States to continue into the future faithfully (particularly

---

9   Francis Howgill, quoted in *Yearly Meeting of the Religious Society of Friends (Quakers) in Britain, Quaker Faith and Practice* (London: Britain Yearly Meeting, 1994), 19.08.

those of European descent), I think we need to go through an Eco-Reformation, an expansion and a breaking open of our vision, a new imaginative landscape in which we can move and grow and hope and transform. As an expansion of the Protestant Reformation, which returned the Christian tradition to a more equitable expression from the hierarchical understanding of the Middle Ages, an Eco-Reformation opens up this faith tradition even further and includes the community of all creation. To participate in this Eco-Reformation, we need to radically reorient our collective life ways from individual control toward collaboration and participation in the community of all life. I'll say that again: we need to radically reorient our collective life ways from individual control toward collaboration and participation in the community of all life. This transformative work intersects with our social and political relationships, our economies, and our spiritual lives, as well as our ecological relationships.

The Lutherans are calling this an Eco-Reformation, and I'll say more about what that means in a few minutes. The work of "rowing on," the theme of annual sessions, is the continued work of recognizing and repenting from the past—that is, letting the Spirit "reveal" to us the truth of our past and present, surrendering our fears and our comfortable habits, and opening ourselves to the Great Turning,[10] the upwelling of the spiritual power I mentioned tapping into a few moments ago. That is the work of Eco-Reformation.

As a way into understanding what I'm talking about

---

10 Joanna Macy and Chris Johnstone, *Active Hope: How to face the mess we're in without going crazy* (Novato, CA: New World Library, 2012), 6.

with an Eco-Reformation, as well as a way to let you know more about me, I'm going to share a bit of my own story of coming to Quakerism and of waking up to the reality of climate justice as the most pressing social justice issue of our time. I think this will help explain the context of my question about whether Quakerism needs to continue, as well as the intersecting nature of climate justice, racial justice, natural resource use, violent conflict, and the beginnings of my own shift in worldview toward an Eco-Reformation.

Born into a Quaker family in Oregon, part of Northwest Yearly Meeting (NWYM), I grew up worshiping in an unprogrammed meeting started by my parents and some of their friends right around the time when I was born. We began attending a programmed Friends meeting when I was about eleven because my parents thought it would be good for me to be in a congregation that had a bigger youth group.

My dad was an important person in my faith journey as a kid, and I remember talking with him often about the big questions of life and faith, spending time hiking, looking at the stars, and engaging in other actions of awe and wonder at the beauty and immensity of this spectacular world.

When I was twelve, my dad let me know one day that he no longer believed in God. So, in my early teen years, I questioned everything about my faith. I questioned the existence of God and whether that God was a personal entity or just some sort of impersonal force. In asking these questions, however, I felt with depth and intensity the presence of an intimately personal Spirit, the epitome of love and care, who was a constant Presence, accompanying me through my questions and doubts. I questioned whether Jesus was the Son of God and whether the Bible is true and/or useful. I felt a deep resonance with the person of Jesus and his way of radical care, and although there are definitely parts of the Bible that are troubling and context-bound, I am grateful for the kindred spirits I find there. The Bible connects me to a long history of people of faith struggling to find meaning, to live faithfully, and to describe and document across time the community's mystical and messy relationship to the Living Spirit of Love.

I questioned whether Quakerism is the right denomination for me, and by this time, I was in high school. I encountered Lucretia Mott, Elizabeth Fry, and John Woolman, and I saw in their words and their work the heart of the gospel message: good news that enacts liberation alongside the oppressed and marginalized. I also experienced the Inward Light of Christ encountered by earlier Friends when I participated in worship, in service, in play, in business meetings, and in youth group. Quakers are my people, and I became a convinced Friend.

Since that time, I have worshiped with programmed Friends in different places in Oregon, as well as sojourns with unprogrammed Friends at Princeton Monthly Meeting when I was working on my master of divinity degree, and South Mountain Friends Meeting in southern Oregon while doing a visiting professorship.

While Friends are still my people, I have also experienced a painful break in my trust in the Quaker process. My yearly meeting removed several meetings over their acknowledgment of queer marriage and ministry. The beautiful vulnerability of seeking the leading of the Spirit together was not honored, and the structures of Quaker process meant that those of us removed from NWYM lost our camps, our college, and much of what we had built together. We created a new yearly meeting that is wonderful, though still hurting, but something beautiful was lost, and the hope and trust of many Friends were broken.

So, that is my story as a Friend and part of what underlies my question of whether Quakerism should continue. Although Quakers are my people, I've seen my people deeply wound one another—not only in my own yearly meeting but also across other parts of our Quaker family; I've seen how Quaker process can be used as a weapon to harm and control and exclude. Are our traditional ways of being Quaker worth renewing, or are they too much a product of European American white supremacy, colonialism, and the ideology of power-over that comes with this worldview? That's a question I think we need to take seriously, and I'm grateful to hear about NEYM's "Noticing Patterns of Oppression and Faithfulness Work Group," which sounds like an attempt to address this systemic problem.

At the same time, I've been seeking and listening about what I am particularly called to work on and what we as Friends need to be focusing on in our time. I was inspired by earlier generations of Friends; I want to be part of my own generation's faithfulness.

As part of my discernment, I went on a delegation with Christian Peacemaker Teams (CPT)[11] to Israel/Palestine in 2008. While I knew a good deal about the conflict there, seeing it with my own eyes brought it home in powerful ways.

---

11   Christian Peacemaker Teams has since changed their name to Community Peacemaker Teams (https://cpt.org/).

One particular evening, I was up late, standing on the rooftop terrace of a Palestinian home in the Dheisheh refugee camp outside Bethlehem. I could see an Israeli settlement, Har Homa, all lit up in its suburban glory on the next hill. I felt angry that Israeli settlers had taken more land from Palestinians, and I was flooded with all the stories we'd heard on the trip: stolen land, intimidated and murdered family members, destruction of olive trees, blockades of water access routes, use of military force against civilians deemed "terrorists" for throwing stones, and petty acts of dehumanization such as using Palestinians' water catch tanks as target practice. I felt righteously angry, and I felt I was on the right side of history, looking down my nose at those who were treating others so unjustly.

And then, I realized that in my own country, it was me in the settlement. Although we're a couple hundred years farther down the road here in our settling of this land in Oregon (and more than that in New England), and we've created laws so that our occupation of this land is considered legal under US law, the situation is the same.[12] My people, European Americans, have claimed all the best land and access to natural resources and dehumanized the Native peoples of these lands in countless ways. Although Friends point to William Penn's purchase of a section of Pennsylvania, most of us do

---

12 In many places across the United States and other parts of the continent, the land was never ceded by Indigenous groups. Additionally, in places where treaties were made, the treaties are often not being followed, and/or treaties were made by small segments of tribal communities without the consent of the whole group. Though the United States considers its actions "legal," this assertion is quite questionable once one begins looking into the bases for these claims.

not live on that fairly purchased land. My Quaker ancestors were some of the first to settle new lands as they moved west with the frontier—but more on that later in the week, when I'll go into a little of what Amanda Kemp talked about in regard to memory and our ability to tell stories of truth and healing about our memories.

What I was experiencing on that terrace in Palestine was awareness of my complicity in colonialism and a recognition of the interconnectedness between colonialism, natural resource exploitation, dehumanizing oppression, injustice, and war. If I'm honest, I went there with a not-well-examined desire to be a white savior, to help bring peace to someone else's conflict. (This is not to speak ill of CPT, and I definitely support their work! But the point is to confess my own complicity in white supremacy and settler colonialist mindsets.)

That night, I realized I was called to stay home, to work on the conflicts and issues in my own place and with my own people. It is my people, European Americans, who others are emulating around the world in land grabs against Indigenous populations, and it is my people who are exerting economic and military control over natural resources and supply chains all over the globe. This was a pivotal moment for me when I began to become aware of the impact of white supremacy and colonialism on my own worldview and on my faith.

So I, like many of you, started being able to see the ways that my life and faith were shaped by my experience as a descendant of colonists, as a citizen of a militarized empire whose main goal is control of other populations and natural resources—even though I grew up Quaker. This was a moment of "revealing," to use the language Noah Merrill introduced in his keynote. I had known about all of this before in my head, but now I *felt* it and knew it to be deeply true about *me*.

There's an interesting healing story in Mark 8:22–25 that feels like an analogy to my experience, so we're going to spend a few minutes with that passage as today's biblical focus.

Mark 8:22–25 comes directly before Mark shows Jesus posing the question, "Who do you say that I am?" to his disciples. This is an important section because it stands at the very heart of Mark's Gospel, between two chunks of teaching and miracle stories. Directly leading up to the climax, the profession of Jesus' Christhood and his explanation of what that means, Mark places this story:

> 22 They came to Bethsaida. Some people brought a blind man to him and begged him to touch him. 23 He took the blind man by the hand and led him out of the village, and when he had put saliva on his eyes and laid his hands on him, he asked him, "Can you see anything?" 24 And the man looked up and said, "I can see people, but they look like trees, walking." 25 Then Jesus laid his hands on his eyes again, and he looked intently, and his sight was restored, and he saw everything clearly. 26 Then he sent him away to his home, saying, "Do not even go into the village."

Nowhere else in the whole Bible do we see Jesus have to touch a person twice in order for them to be healed. At first glance, it seems like a story where Jesus fails, but that misses the point. Mark isn't showing Jesus as an incompetent healer, but he's showing the *followers* of Jesus their inability to see clearly. The story of the healing of this man was likely a story Mark inherited from oral tradition, but he places it at this point in his gospel for a very specific reason: it serves as a metaphor about what needs to happen to the disciples.

This becomes clear when we look at the stories right around this miracle. The story right before this shows the disciples not really "seeing" what Jesus means when he tells them to beware the yeast of the Pharisees and Herod: they think he's getting on their case for forgetting to bring bread. He asks them, "Why are you talking about having no bread? Do you still not perceive or understand? Are your hearts hardened? Do you have eyes and fail to see? Do you have ears and fail to hear? And do you not remember?" (Mark 8:17–18). Rather than talking about actual bread, he's using the idea of yeast metaphorically: the ideas and attitudes of the Pharisees and Herod, their concerns with political power, influence, and wealth can work their way through the "dough" of the faith community. The disciples completely miss his point regarding the potential damage that can be done when faith leaders focus on the mindset of material and political blessings as a mark of God's favor.

Then, right after the passage about the healing of the man who was blind, Jesus asks them who others and who they themselves think Jesus is: they say they think he's the Christ—but they don't really "see" him for who he is. They recognize Jesus as important, probably even unparalleled among prophets. They've left everything and followed him. They think he's the Messiah, the one they've been waiting for.

But even though the disciples understand all this, they aren't really seeing fully what and who Jesus is—they're still seeing people looking like trees walking around. Jesus explains to them what it means that he is the Christ in Mark 8:31: he's the Son of Humanity who must suffer and die—and he explains this again in chapter 9 and a third time in chapter 10. Even though Jesus explains this repeatedly, the disciples still expect the Christ to be a triumphant military leader who will wipe out the Romans and re-establish the throne of Israel—they expect this even up to Jesus' arrest and death. They see more clearly than they ever have before! But they are still expecting Jesus to establish a political empire.

In the story of the healing of this man, there are several things that might help us see how this metaphor applies to us. First, Jesus takes him by the hand and leads him outside the village. This may have been unknown territory for the blind man, who gets around by feel and spatial memory, which is easier within a town than out in the open. Jesus takes the man someplace where he is not comfortable, but he is leading him by the hand.

Jesus touches his eyes and then asks, "Can you see anything?" The man *can* see something: he sees people who look like trees. If I had been in this situation, I could imagine myself being ecstatic that I could actually *see* something! I might be tempted to jump up, saying, "Thank you, and of course, I can see something," and run off, assuming people are *supposed* to look like trees walking around. But this man listens to Jesus' question, tells him what he sees, and waits while Jesus touches him again. Then his eyes are fully restored, and he can see clearly.

Additionally, it's important to see this man as a whole and worthy person regardless of whether he had clear sight. Though in that time and place, he was treated as an outsider by the community because of his perceived imperfection, that was a choice of the community, not a deficiency in the man experiencing blindness. Healing and restoration into the community happened in this case because Jesus healed his eyes, but it could equally have happened through the community being inclusive enough that he would have been a full member without physical healing.[13]

I recognize myself in the experience of this man, and I also see this as a metaphor for us as a community of Friends. Perhaps we have experienced partial spiritual healing, but maybe we are in need of a second healing touch. We are also the community in need of Jesus' healing touch so we can recognize our need to live in such a way that each one has a place of belonging in our collective body.

What I experienced in Palestine was something like that

---

13 I add this paragraph with gratitude to Greg Woods, who spoke this important addition to the message during waiting worship. See also scholars discussing disability theology as an interdependence theology, which has important implications as we live into an Eco-Reformation in which we recognize our interconnectedness with all other parts of creation, contrary to the white supremacist notion of independence, e.g.: Deborah Creamer, "Theological Accessibility: The Contribution of Disability," *Disability Studies Quarterly* 26, no. 4 (2006); Paul Leshota, "From dependence to interdependence: Towards a practical theology of disability," *HTS Teologiese Studies/Theological Studies* 71, no. 2 (2015): 01–09, doi.org/10.4102/HTS.V71I2.2680. See also the final section of this booklet, "A Quaker Ecology: Our Bodies as Fractals of Hope."

second touch of Jesus, where I realized that although I had been seeing some things, I had not been seeing clearly. Jesus took him outside the village to a place where he was uncomfortable, just like my experience. I think we can also have these kinds of experiences without having to go to a foreign country. We can sit with an idea or a perspective that we haven't encountered before, and we can allow our worldview to be opened up, clarified, or expanded.

Regardless of who you think Jesus was, he was encouraging his disciples to see him more clearly, and that meant they knew he was going to suffer and die. To be his disciple meant then (and means now) following him on that path that leads us out of our comfort zones into something life-altering.

Also, while it can feel convicting and possibly shaming to recognize the ways our actions have not been rightly focused in the past, using this passage as a metaphor hopefully opens us up to our need—a clarifying of our vision rather than something shameful to try to conceal.

This second healing touch and the encouragement to form communities of belonging amidst difference provide a metaphor for the Eco-Reformation I want to describe next. An Eco-Reformation is an expansion of our understanding of some of the main ideas of the original Reformation. As Friends, we are like the man in the story: we recognize that we can now see in part—we as Friends have lived into Jesus' vision of the good news of God's kin-dom in many ways—but we do not see as clearly as we could. We are still in need of more healing.

What I'm proposing as an Eco-Reformation is a reorientation of our worldview that expands and clarifies what we already know to be true as Friends, but we're going to need a second spiritual healing touch in order to get there. The Eco-Reformation takes into account the reality of our embodiedness within creation, with the opportunity and necessity of living in ways that contribute to planetary flourishing. While individual choices to purchase more sustainable items and reduce our emissions are a necessary part of the work that needs to be done, our individual purchase choices are nowhere near sufficient to get us to where we need to be to leave a livable planet to future generations. For the Quaker denomination to continue faithfully into the twenty-first century, we need to accept this second healing touch, which will mean a radical reorientation of most of our spiritual, social, and economic lives. Are we up for it?

I am going to assume we want to be up for continuing the Quaker denomination into the twenty-first century and beyond, not just in a way that recapitulates our institutions but in a way that continues to focus each of us on the Light of Christ that drew in early Friends and speaks to us today. I am assuming we want to continue to practice Quakerism in ways that are relevant, not for the sake of popularity but for the purpose of drawing deeply from our spiritual wells to remind our societies to act faithfully in the current time. To do this, I propose that we need to engage in an Eco-Reformation. So, what would this Eco-Reformation look like? It is this question that we will be exploring together in the rest of this booklet. I will conclude this first section with a few definitions that will help set the stage for that work.

First, what do I mean by Eco-Reformation? Historian Phillip Watson described the Protestant Reformation in the

1500s as a "Copernican Revolution" in religion: people's whole worldview shifted as dramatically as it did when scientists realized we orbit the sun rather than the sun orbiting us.[14] In the Protestant Reformation, we shifted our cultural understanding of responsibility for our faith from a transaction with a priest to a relationship between ourselves and God: a priesthood of all believers—and of course, Friends took that even further.

In an Eco-Reformation, another shift in worldview is necessary. The book *Eco-Reformation: Grace and Hope for a Planet in Peril* describes this shift: "To address the eco-crises we face, we also need to conceive anew what it means to be human. We have imagined ourselves living *on* the Earth rather than embedded in it and thoroughly dependent on it. We have focused on the well-being of humans to the neglect of the well-being of all living things."[15] In this moment, we are seeing the effects of the Reformation's imperfect vision of an individualized religion and the parallel societal impacts of the Enlightenment and modernism, which have centered human beings as "subjects" while all other parts of creation are "objects"—and of course, certain human beings are seen as more reliable or important "subjects" in our culture that has centered the white, male, cisgender, heterosexual, European-American experience as normative.

The shift in worldview required by the Eco-Reformation can be visualized in this helpful graphic that shows the

---

14 Lisa E. Dahill and James B. Martin-Schramm, eds., *Eco-Reformation: Grace and Hope for a Planet in Peril* (Eugene, OR: Cascade Books, 2017), 4.
15 Dahill & Martin-Schramm, 11.

difference between an "ego" and an "eco" perspective.[16] The "ego" perspective is based on the Western worldview, where there is a hierarchy, a Great Chain of Being,[17] that extends from God to (male) human beings to other human beings in a rigid hierarchy to animals that are similar to humans, to other animals, to plants, and so forth. In this schema, the land is seen as a set of commodities, as "objects" to be used for the sake of human beings, important for their utility to us, and able to be quantified by their market value.

In the "eco" perspective, humanity is part of the whole. Rather than hierarchical, this model is relational. Each individual, species, and landscape element holds a unique and vital place in a web of relations. This web breaks down the *illusion* of hierarchy and individuality: human beings cannot

---

16 Ego-Eco graphic by Steffen Lehmann, 2010, creative commons license 4.0.

17 An idea first developed by Plato, the concept of a Great Chain of Being was further explicated by Plotinus in Neoplatonic thought. This idea supported the view of order for the Medieval church and feudal hierarchies, as well as the foundational understandings of Enlightenment thought and science such as the classification of species created by Carl Linnaeus. John W. Cooper, *Panentheism–The Other God of the Philosophers: From Plato to the Present* (Grand Rapids, MI: Baker Publishing Group, 2006); Arthur O. Lovejoy, *The Great Chain of Being: A Study of the History of an Idea* (United Kingdom: Taylor & Francis Group, 2017).

exist without the plants and animals that nourish them, without the land that tethers them in place through gravity, without water and sunlight, without the microscopic gut flora that digest our food and make up our microbiome—some estimate that about half our cells are bacteria.[18] Even in our own bodies, we are a community of life, and we rely on the interconnected web of our global community in order to live on this planet.

Part of the necessary shift is learning to see and interpret our history, our sacred text, and our own lives through the lens of this Eco-Reformation. To do this, we can make use of ecological hermeneutics as well as decolonizing hermeneutics. Therefore, some definitions are in order: hermeneutics is just a fancy word for interpretation. Interpreting the Bible through an ecological and decolonizing lens means that we read scripture with awareness of the current ecological crisis and its compounding of racial and other injustices, and we attend to ways in which the biblical text breaks down the ideas of colonialism, empire-building, and the impulses of control and domination.[19] We also have to be aware that the biblical text has been used to support colonization and oppression, so those of us from people groups who have benefited from oppressive interpretations have to use care when

18   R. Sender, S. Fuchs, and R. Milo, "Revised Estimates for the Number of Human and Bacteria Cells in the Body," *PLoS biology* 14, no. 8 (2016): e1002533, https://doi.org/10.1371/journal.pbio.1002533.

19   Norman C. Habel and Peter L. Trudinger, eds., *Exploring Ecological Hermeneutics, Symposium Series no. 46.* (Atlanta: Society of Biblical Literature, 2008); S. D. Moore and F. F. Segovia, eds., *Postcolonial biblical criticism: Interdisciplinary intersections* (NewYork: T.&T.Clark, 2005).

approaching biblical interpretation, making sure we are open to our received interpretations being challenged and broken down as we encounter readings of these texts by people who have been traditionally oppressed.

An ecological and decolonizing hermeneutic emerges as we use this critical and open approach, listening to the liberating Spirit of God speaking through biblical texts and listening to others who can help us shift our interpretations. When we start paying attention to the way the land and other creatures are part of the story, we see the heart of the biblical witness pointing toward a participatory community of all life.

As I pointed out in regard to the passage from Mark, Jesus' disciples expected him to build an empire. Instead, he made it known that they needed to get their vision checked again: he was *not* about building empires. So this is an example of using a decolonizing hermeneutic to open up the biblical text to help us really *see* the work of the Eco-Reformation. Further, recognizing the man in the story, though blind, already had a place of belonging in Jesus' community can help us begin to understand an ecological perspective of theology, including interconnectedness and inherent value, where each one is included despite—or even because of—our unique place in the biodiversity that makes up the global community.

As a human species and particularly as individuals from the United States, we have this choice before us: to live into an ecological worldview or to continue to operate under an egoic worldview until we exhaust all the planet's gifts. This is a very real and stark choice faced by us all, Quaker or not. For Friends to continue to have a meaningful role in the coming decades and centuries, we must make a choice to move fully into that ecological worldview now, altering unjust and unsustainable systems and moving into new ways of acknowledging our relatedness.

Therefore, I return us to the queries I posed earlier: Does Quakerism need to continue? If so, what would a faithful Friends community look like in this century?

I continue to have hope that Friends can connect deeply to the truest and most courageous parts of our tradition and move into this Eco-Reformation in the transformative power of the Present Spirit.

2. Incarnation and a Quaker Ecotheology of Light

Light, as a metaphor grounded in scripture and beloved by many across different branches of the Friends tradition, forms a possible starting point for a particularly Quaker ecotheology.[20] This can help us form a theoretical basis for a move into an Eco-Reformation, stemming from the wisdom of our own tradition. This metaphor can orient us and open our imaginations to new ways of relating to others, creation, and God through the Quaker metaphor of the Inward Light and the text of John 1.

Section 1 discussed the need for an Eco-Reformation, where our understanding of ourselves and the human role moves from an individual, "ego," hierarchical perspective to an "eco" perspective, where we see ourselves as participants in the ongoing co-creation of the community of all life. If Quakerism has a meaningful role in the coming decades, we will need to participate in this Eco-Reformation. I used the story from Mark 8 of the man who was partially healed of his blindness with Jesus' first healing touch, suggesting the first Reformation may have gotten us part of the way in seeing Jesus' way clearly, but we need to be open to a "second touch" as Friends. That second touch opens us, particularly those of us who are of European heritage, to a new clarity regarding the ways the Western empire and the myth of white supremacy have infiltrated our theology and our Quaker systems and

---

20   A book on this subject will be released shortly: Cherice Bock and Christy Randazzo, *Quakers, Ecology, and the Light*, Brill Research Perspectives in Quaker Studies, Brill Research Perspectives in Humanities and Social Sciences Series, forthcoming.

that these attitudes have caused a situation of profound danger in terms of how we utilize the resources of creation, as well as the ways we oppress people and other species. Can we go through the necessary work of this Eco-Reformation as a community? This is partially the work of imagination, letting ourselves dream big as we envision the shift we are in the middle of going through.

We can begin that work by reimagining our understanding of the Inward Light, and this section will analyze and reexamine the text of John 1. My hope is to give us a particularly Quaker entry point into the shift toward an ecological worldview that is required in an Eco-Reformation.

> 1 In the beginning was the Word, and the Word was with God, and the Word was God. 2 The Word was in the beginning with God. 3 All things came into being through the Word, and without the Word not one thing came into being. What has come into being 4 in the Word was life, and the life was the light of all people. 5 The light shines in the darkness, and the darkness did not overcome it. 6 There was a man sent from God, whose name was John. 7 He came as a witness to testify to the light, so that all might believe through him. 8 He himself was not the light, but he came to testify to the light. 9 The true light, which enlightens everyone, was coming into the world. 10 He was in the world, and the world came into being through him; yet the world did not know him. 11 He came to what was his own, and his own people did not accept him. 12

But to all who received him, who believed in his name, he gave power to become children of God, 13 who were born, not of blood or of the will of the flesh or of the will of man, but of God. 14 And the Word became flesh and lived among us, and we have seen his glory, the glory as of a father›s only son, full of grace and truth.

I will hazard a guess that this is a favorite passage of many Friends, perhaps a close second to John 15, where our denominational name comes from. In this passage, the Word and the Light come into the world, becoming flesh in Jesus. The eternal Presence that was with God and was God chooses to enter creation in a unique way.

While this passage is beloved by many Friends, it is also the source of some of our most enduring controversies about the nature of Jesus. I hope that, no matter what your perspective on Jesus' identity, you can open yourself to that perspective being challenged and expanded.

John 1 is an important passage for developing an ecological worldview based in the Bible, particularly a Quaker one. By understanding the meaning of John 1 in relation to Greek philosophical ideas popular at the time, we can gain a better understanding of what the author of John was trying to indicate about Jesus: by describing a God who entered material reality, the author of John is rejecting the idea that the material world is evil, but as will be made clear in what follows, the author was showing that Jesus' message was antithetical to the ideas of earthly power structures based on power-over and control. I will unpack John by reading it through an ecological and decolonizing lens, and then I will discuss how this reading shifts and expands our Quaker understanding of the Inward Light.

In this passage, Jesus is described as the Divine Logos, the Word, as well as the life-bringing Light. In the context of that time period, the author of John was both connecting the Jesus Movement to the Greek philosophical tradition and challenging that tradition. He was drawing together Hebrew and Greek cosmologies or understandings of the cosmos. To get a sense of what the author was doing in his own time period so that we can interpret the passage in its context and in our own time, it is necessary to explain the main aspects of Greek philosophy to which the author of John was responding.

In Greek philosophical tradition, the Logos or Word was considered the ultimate essence of reason, order, and logic. Some Greek philosophers equated the Logos with God. The Logos is that which gives meaning to the cosmos, the original Word that symbolizes all thought and communication. Light was closely associated with the Logos: as in the Enlightenment, light was seen as a metaphor for that which opens up our understanding. It is the source of life, so its essential quality is "source." This understanding of the concepts of Logos and Light was influenced by Plato and continued to be developed through Aristotle and other Platonists. The basic idea was that there were essential forms that exist as abstract concepts but cannot exist in their absolute sense in the material world. For example, imagine a sphere. You can imagine a perfect sphere that is completely smooth, and the diameter is consistent no matter where you slice it along its central point. In real life, however, there is no way to create such a form.

This led to dualism: the concept (or abstract object) is the ideal, whereas the material world can only be an imperfect grasping toward that ideal. In much of Greek thought and religious expressions, therefore, the material world was seen as less-than, while the world of the Logos, the spiritual and rational realm, was considered disconnected from the material world and was an ideal to reach for. In the several centuries after Jesus, this hierarchical dualism between matter and spirit developed into Gnosticism and Neoplatonism, and we can see the beginnings of this controversy being addressed throughout the Bible. On the one hand, biblical authors define the evil parts of the world and the benefits of a spiritual perspective, while they also place a strong emphasis on the goodness of creation and our embodied existence.

The next strand of this section will focus on the Word or Logos invoked in John 1, which helps connect the Jesus Movement to Greek philosophy. This connection to Greek philosophy helped make sense of Jesus' message to potential new followers, which was important, as Jesus' disciples were spreading his message around the Greek-speaking world, but it was only a qualified connection because the platonic ideals can lead to a dualism of matter and spirit that is not consistent with the message of Jesus.

According to the text of John 1, the Word (Logos) was pre-existent, and through it, the work of creation was conceived and birthed (John 1:1–3): the Word is also the Light, bringer of life (John 1:4). The Light overpowers darkness (John 1:5). John the Baptist was a prophet that could speak of the Light, but was not himself the Light (John 1:19–28). So far, the passage is consistent with Greek ideals.

But then, something strange and potentially heretical to Greek thought happens: the text moves from talking about the Light as an "it" (the word for light in Greek is neuter, without gender) to talking about "he." In verse 9, it says, "The light, the true one, the one who gives light to all people, was coming into the world," and it switches to masculine pronouns in verse 10: "He was in the world." The reader would have been wondering who this "he" is. Then things get really challenging for the Greek worldview: this preexistent Logos and true Light becomes flesh and is born and pitches his tent among us in verse 14. (The word translated "dwell," σκηνοω, *skeno-o*, more literally means "pitches a tent" or "to dwell in a tent.") In essence, this eternal ideal comes camping with us, pitching a tent, incarnating in a human form, and hangs out with us for a while in the midst of creation.

This challenges the Greek notion of the material world being evil or a place to be avoided. In many of the other religious traditions swirling around in that time period, an eternal, essential God could not actually come in contact with matter because matter was evil. It was necessary to try to escape and negate one's material desires and needs as much as possible in order to seek the spiritual. John's Gospel starts right off by challenging this dualism. The material world is not evil; instead, God—the preexistent Logos—can incarnate in a body, one which communicates the true Light powerfully to the world.

When we read this passage using an ecological and decolonizing lens, a few things stand out. The first and most

34

important is the part about the Incarnation: our word for incarnation comes from the Latin, meaning "in the flesh." The eternal ideal of logic and spiritual truth became a participant in creation, fully fleshed, birthed by a woman in all the messiness that surrounds childbirth and which was often considered unclean.[21] Jesus, according to the text, comes in the flesh, camping with us for a time, and he is the embodiment of the ideal—and in so doing, he completely breaks open the Greek understanding of that ideal.

In the Greek ideal, matter and Logos could not meet, and the goal was to escape material reality to live mostly on the plane of ideas and spiritual attunement. This is an idea that has also greatly influenced our entire Western cultural,

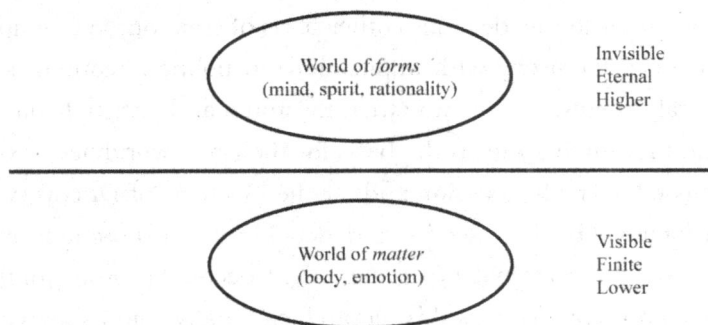

World of *forms*
(mind, spirit, rationality)

Invisible
Eternal
Higher

World of *matter*
(body, emotion)

Visible
Finite
Lower

---

21 I will also point out here, in a feminist reading, that the text says "not out of the desire or will of any man," and it does not use the gender inclusive word *anthropos*, it uses the word for a man, *aner*. This was not a plan dreamed up or able to be controlled by any man. Instead it was a generative work of co-creation.

God

Culture
Spirit
Intellect
Subject

Man

Women
Children
People of Color
Animals
Nature

Nature
Emotion
Resources
Property
Object

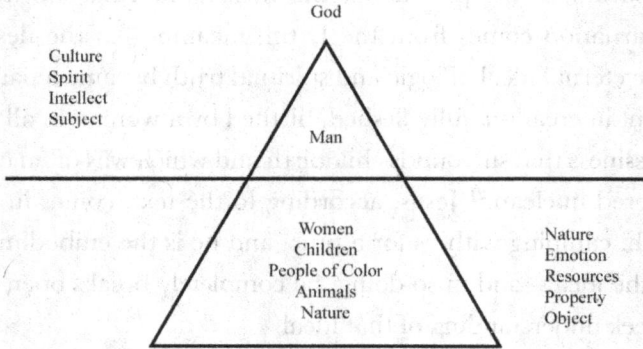

philosophical, and religious tradition, setting up a dualistic hierarchy wherein men are considered more "rational" and therefore closer to the ideal than women, Westerners (read: whites) are considered more civilized and therefore closer to the ideal than people from other cultures, Christians are closer to the ideal than non-Christians, and human beings are closer to the ideal than other parts of creation, setting up a social hierarchy with implications in politics, economics, legal systems, and the way we think about and distribute natural resources. This is the basis for the egoic worldview discussed in the first session and for the Doctrine of Discovery, which will be discussed in more detail in the next section. By showing the eternal Word and Light becoming flesh, John 1 completely destroys this hierarchical dualism and shows a God who is relational and participatory.

Also, in addition to opening up the Greek worldview, this challenged the assumptions of the Jewish religious leadership of Jesus' day in relation to their understanding of the Messiah. As discussed in the first section, Mark's Jesus shows the disciples that they are only seeing his true nature in part:

they had idealized the Messiah as someone who would come and take over the throne of David and establish an empire through military might. In this passage in John 1, the author is setting up his response to that assumption, showing Jesus as Messiah *and* as so much more than just a military ruler who will establish a new nation of Israel. Instead, he is a pre-existent part of God, and he came to his own, but his own did not recognize him. Obviously, Jesus himself was a Jew, and many Jews *did* recognize him as the Messiah, so this is *not* to say that his own people didn't recognize him in that way, but that many of those who held the power of interpreting the scriptures in his community did not recognize him because they were expecting an empire builder.

So the first important thing we notice about this passage is that it both fits with and challenges Greek and Hebrew understandings: the material world can be and is infused with the ideal of the Logos and the Light, with the Word made flesh, born, walking around, and dying, completely participating in the messiness of creation. And although the Messiah is completely in the flesh and participating in everything that goes along with being human, he is not an imperial ruler who will play into the egoic hierarchy of domination and control by restoring Israel's earthly monarchy; rather, he camps out among us, showing his glory to those who can sense it, but many of those with "authority" in religious circles do not recognize him because they themselves are participating in the worldview of domination and control.

The second thing we can notice when reading John 1 from an ecological and decolonizing perspective is the use of the word "world." The word translated "world" in verses

9–10 is *kosmos*; he came into the *kosmos*, and he had created the *kosmos*, but the *kosmos* did not recognize him. This can come across as implying that "the world" was completely unable to comprehend the Logos, so perhaps the Greek understanding of the separation between spirit and matter would be able to be supported if the world is assumed to be the material world in general. While the term *kosmos* is sometimes used to mean something similar to our understanding of the "cosmos," as in the whole universe or the interstellar expanses, it often has the connotation in the Bible of "worldly affairs" and implies a system of order. When Jesus says in John 18:36 that his kingdom is not of "this world," he uses this term to mean that his kingdom is not related to the ways that the worldly authorities set up their affairs; it is not a military endeavor or a political party. So here, in John 1:9–10, the systems that order human affairs did not recognize Jesus: those with political and religious power, those who benefited from the empire of their day, are the *kosmos*, and they did not know the Word or recognize the Light in Jesus.

There are two other important words in Greek that are not present in this passage but that can help us get a sense of what the author is *not* saying about the material world here. The first is *ktisis*, meaning creation. You may recall that in Genesis 1, God created everything and called it good. In the third section of this booklet, this term will be important in regard to Romans 8, which indicates all of creation participates in the work God is doing of reconciling all things. Creation is good, and it is a part of the story, not just a backdrop for human experience. In other words, creation is different from what the author of John is talking about here as "the world."

The second word I want to explain is *oikumene*, which means the entire world in the sense of the planet we inhabit. This term comes from the root *oikos*, meaning "household," and *oikos* is also the root of our English words with the prefix "eco," as in ecology and economy.[22] You might say *oikumene* is the Earth community, the place where life happens, and it is intensely communal, implying a household, a relational network. The main distinction I am drawing here is that the term *kosmos* has more to do with the powers and principalities of the world, the structures that are set up to order human affairs, but the term *kosmos* does not refer to the material world in general. Creation is good, and the planet is our household, the place in which we live and relate to God and show love for our neighbors.

When the Word and Light became incarnate and pitched his tent among us, he did so in the *oikumene*, and although the *kosmos* did not recognize him, this does not mean creation or the material world is evil. Far from it: Jesus showed us an example of how to live within the *oikumene* while resisting the harmful aspects of the *kosmos*, the systems and structures of power, the ways that worldly authorities try to control and dominate. He embodied the life-giving Light and Word that can create and co-create, that can go camping with us and smash the patriarchy with us, that can speak the Divine Word into our deepest longings for meaning and that can reconcile us to our embodied selves in all our mess of lived experience.

To summarize, when read through an ecological and

---

22   The concept of *oikos* will be returned to in sections 3 and 5.

decolonizing lens, John 1 shows us that the eternal Word and Light is intimately connected and incarnated into creation, and although the systems and powers of this world do not recognize Jesus' embodiment of the Divine Way, he is offering us a "pattern," an "example,"[23] of what it looks like to participate fully in the ecology—the household—of creation.

While this understanding of John 1 is important for anyone who is seeking to participate in the Eco-Reformation, you may be wondering what is particularly Quaker about it, so we will discuss that next. Since Friends have connected with the concept of the Inward Light, exploring this passage helps us find a particularly Quaker entry point into the Eco-Reformation. Exploring the concept of the Light can also help us notice places in our own tradition where we have missed the point of what John—and Jesus—were saying, where we have lived comfortably with the *kosmos* rather than equitably in the community of creation. Developing an ecotheology of light may help Friends expand on our tradition's beautiful and meaningful metaphor of the Inward Light so that it is not only a mystical, spiritual experience but so that it also includes our embodied experience.

In my observation and experience, Quakers have often fallen into the dualistic problems I explained in regard to Western thought, where we think of the spiritual and the rational or intellectual—the Logos—as more important than the material. We have a tendency to try escaping our embodied form by practicing silent, internal worship. While we do have a pretty good track record of our contemplative style

---

23 Fox, *Journal*, 263.

of worship grounding us in the courage and moral fortitude to take stands for social justice, which relates to the material world, in my experience, our understanding of the Inward Light is often focused on individual mystical encounter and may or may not be connected to engagement with a participatory community, be that human or beyond human.

John 1 begins with the eternal Word and explains that the Word is the creator—and what it was creating is life, "and the life was the light of all people." While John the Baptist was able to testify to that Light, Jesus embodied it and made it accessible to "all who receive him," and this occurred through incarnation into a body, a body that dwelled on this planet and interacted with people and other parts of creation. This was not just a metaphorical light, a spiritual light that opens us up to a mystical realm where we can escape from our bodily existence. Instead, this is a Light that is intimately connected to life, the living, breathing, birthing, and dying life without which none of us can experience God—or anything else for that matter, since we have to exist in bodies, at least for this earthly part of our journey.

I propose we expand our Quaker understanding of the Inward Light to not only refer to our personal spiritual experience but to also include our connectedness to all the rest of the life on planet Earth and in our solar system and the universe. So the Inward Light is partial vision, but we need that second healing touch[24] to see more fully how the Light is at work. I will explain what this expanded view of the Light means theologically and how our usual understandings of the Light sometimes lead us back to an egoic view of the world.

---

24 Discussed in section 1.

When we reframe our understanding of the Light, it can help us truly *see* into an Eco-Reformation.

Light from the sun literally makes it possible for there to be life on this planet. If you think of the ecosystem in which you live, most of the species rely directly on light to grow and be nourished, and the species that do not receive the direct effects of light because they are underground, receive the indirect effects by working to decompose things that were once nourished by light and by creating underground networks to transfer energy from the sun from one being to another. All life on this planet is supported and connected by the sun's life-giving energy moving through the ecosystem. Light is the current and the currency moving through the entire *oikos*—the ecosystem and the economy, and it allows us each to participate in the whole process. We are all related to each other in our reliance on the light as well as our different ways of processing and experiencing that light so that we can ideally collaborate together toward a system in which each one receives the light we need, gives out of our abundance, and each has a niche and a purpose that is unique and needed by the whole.

The understanding of the Inward Light that is sometimes communicated by Friends can prop up a hierarchical, egoic worldview within Quakerism, where we think of each person as an individual connecting with the Light, and we think of ourselves as human beings as special in our ability to access that Light compared to other species. By expanding our understanding of the Light from one of personal experience to an ecosystem model, where the Light connects us to all other life, we become participants in the co-labor of

life-making. We move from a worldview of trying to dominate and control the world around us to one of partnership
and collaboration, working together across the *oikumene*, the
global household.

An egoic understanding of the Inward Light can easily
become competitive, where my understanding of the Light
must "win" by controlling or dominating, by convincing you
of my authority to interpret the Light, or simply by being my
interpretation that is disconnected from yours or from its real-
world impacts. This sounds to me, however, quite similar to
the *kosmos*, the worldly authorities who did not recognize the
incarnation of the Divine Light, who tried to control Jesus
and the interpretation of scripture in ways that kept in place
the status quo of their religious and political systems to privilege themselves. Our appeals to the guidance of the Inward
Light, when practiced from this egoic perspective, can end up
in the same place: reproducing the systems of white supremacy, overuse of natural resources, and competitive economic
models that only benefit a few.

An ecotheology of Light reminds us of our relatedness to
one another and to the rest of creation. It also emphasizes
humility: we are a species that can respond to the Light, but
we are not the only one. An ecotheology of Light reorients
us from the *kosmos* emphasis on order, expressed harmfully
through requirements of uniformity, to an emphasis on
diversity. In an ecosystem, all parts are needed, and each
species and individual within that ecosystem contributes
a piece that could not be contributed by anyone else. The
kosmos model creates acres and acres of single monocrops and
replicates strip malls across the country and world with the

same stores; it creates factories where the machine parts, as well as the human workers, are interchangeable. It creates "law and order," where the laws perpetuate the status quo, and the "order" is the *Pax Romana*, the government-sanctioned violent quelling of resistance. The ecotheology of Light celebrates biodiversity and creativity. It is flexible and adaptive, resilient in the face of change, and works with the planet's natural cycles of more and less light, as well as different ecosystem successionary stages in the case of fire, storm, volcano, or other natural occurrence. Within this model, each individual relies on the others in the ecosystem to nourish one another as we process the Light in different ways. We go through seasons and cycles, we are open to birth and death, we participate in periods of growth and decomposition, we recognize our own and our community's limits, and we live within them with gratitude and flourishing.

Just as Jesus' rejection of the harmful interpretations of the religious leaders of his day did not mean he was saying "anything goes," an ecotheology of Light points us back to the life-giving laws that sustain us, that help us to live as a community. These laws look different in each context—each individual grows differently and is formed by their geographical location. The amount of light each receives is different based on where they are on the planet and the actions of other individuals around them. Ecosystems are always changing and growing; there is no such thing as eternal stasis or equilibrium—ecosystems are living and dynamic. The natural laws create space for unique ways of flourishing to occur and for diversity to emerge in all its glory.

When I titled this booklet, "A Quaker Ecology: Meditations on the Future of Friends," this is the Quaker ecology I have in mind. If Friends are to have a faithful future, I believe it will be in this direction, moving from our tendency as a Society of Friends in the United States to get caught up in systems that perpetuate white supremacy and ecological degradation, toward participation in the community of all life.

In the next section, we will discuss the implications of participating as members in this community of all life, compared to our attempts to try pretending we are outside that community, controlling it, and claiming all the Light's benefits for our own species and our own people groups. This is spiritual work that requires us to act as fully embodied persons, carrying the spark of the Divine Light that we can recognize at work in each one and allowing the Divine to touch us a second time to clear our vision so we can see how to participate in the ecotheology of Light in which we are embedded.

3. Watershed Discipleship: Repentance, Re-membering, and Reinhabiting

A few years ago, I experienced a beautiful liturgy written by one of my Lutheran minister friends called "The River's Lament" about the Willamette River.[25] It told the story of the Willamette, the river's parents, the local mountains; and her grandmother, the ocean. The lament told of her relationship to the people groups who lived in what is now Oregon before Europeans arrived, and then it told the story of what had happened to her, the river, in the last 200 years since Europeans came. From controlling her curves and her flow with dams and floodwalls, to dumping raw sewage, to even more toxic chemicals used for industrial purposes, this lament cut me straight to the heart. I have lived within a few miles of the Willamette River most of my life, and when I was a kid, I played in a little creek that forms a tributary of the river. I spent time boating and water skiing with friends on the Willamette as a teen, and we always made fun of how dirty the water was and how there were probably three-eyed fish from all the toxins.

When I heard "The River's Lament," I woke up to the idea of the river as an entity, as a being with a history, a story, a voice. My whole attitude toward her shifted: I started calling her my sister, and I apologized for making fun of

---

25 Rev. Solveig Nilsen-Goodin and others in the Wilderness Way Community composed "The River's Lament," a series of stations along the Bluff on the University of Portland campus, overlooking the Portland Harbor Superfund Site. Though it is not published or available online in full text, you can read more about it at the EcoFaith Recovery website: http://www.ecofaithrecovery.org/events-2/the-rivers-lament/.

her. Although I have not done a lot to help return her to her former glory, I recently have been able to join the Portland Harbor Collaborative Group, which exists to hold accountable the polluting groups and the Environmental Protection Agency for the cleanup of the Portland Harbor Superfund Site.[26]

This experience of "The River's Lament," as well as reading Robin Wall Kimmerer's *Braiding Sweetgrass*, were turning points for me in recognizing other parts of creation as subjects and not as objects to be used as natural resources. The chapter that really got me was called "Learning the Grammar of Animacy," in which Kimmerer describes how her Anishinaabe people's language, Potawatomi, shifted her way of relating to other beings in the world. Rather than dividing up language by gender and by subject/object, actor and acted upon, in Potawatomi, entities are described as living or nonliving. Living entities include ones we think of as "inanimate" in English, such as rocks, songs, drums, and stories, while inanimate things are generally made by people. As Kimmerer puts it:

> A bay is a noun only if water is *dead*. When *bay* is a noun, it is defined by humans, trapped between its shores, and contained by the word. But the verb *wiikwegamaa*—to *be* a bay—releases the water from bondage and lets it live. "To be a

---

26 Learn more about the Portland Harbor, the Superfund Site, and the Collaborative Group at this website, and read stories (including mine) in the "Local Stories" tab: "Portland Harbor Superfund Site," Environmental Protection Agency website, https://storymaps.arcgis.com/stories/ab89faf239624854a5b9c7723f1c43da.

bay" holds the wonder that, for this moment, the living water has decided to shelter itself between these shores, conversing with cedar roots and a flock of baby mergansers. Because it could do otherwise—become a stream or an ocean or a waterfall, and there are verbs for that, too. *This* is the language I hear in the woods; this is the language that lets us speak of what wells up all around us.[27]

I think many of you can feel that language that "lets us speak of what wells up all around us," too—it's something we are not exactly taught in Western cultures, and the English language does not help us much. It is something that we are sometimes attuned to as Friends. We do not have words for it, but we can recognize the living Spirit, the Light, at work in our midst during gathered meetings for worship and in the creatures around us. Even the stones can cry out for justice, right (Habakkuk 2:11; Luke 19:40)? And the trees clap their hands, and the stars praise God, and the heavens declare God's glory (Isaiah 55:12; Psalm 148:3; Psalm 19:1). In English, we tend to think of these ideas from the Hebrew scriptures as anthropomorphism, as applying human characteristics to other entities, and with our supposedly superior, rational minds, we see these as metaphors. Or we can look back and see, in our own tradition's sacred text, this grammar of animacy at work, reminding us of our relatedness to the rest of creation that I had to rediscover in my sister, the Willamette River.

---

27   Robin Wall Kimmerer, *Braiding Sweetgrass: Indigenous Wisdom, Scientific Knowledge and the Teachings of Plants* (Minneapolis, MN: Milkweed Editions, 2013), 55.

The title for this section is "Watershed Discipleship: Repentance, Re-membering, and Reinhabiting." Section 2 was about Light, and this section is mostly about land and water, including colonization and our responsibility to descendants of earlier inhabitants of Turtle Island. Part of the work of the Eco-Reformation introduced in the first section requires consciously being disciples in our places, in our watersheds. This includes re-membering ourselves as participants in the community of creation and re-membering our stories, including the stories in the Bible. This opens up space for us to reclaim portions of the text where an ecological and decolonizing hermeneutic can be discerned, as well as critiquing parts of our biblical, denominational, and personal stories that have missed the mark in regard to treatment of land and other creatures. After sharing about the biblical threads of care for creation, I will re-member with you some of my own story as an example.

As we do this work of Eco-Reformation, which is to say, "primitive Christianity revived again,"[28] watershed discipleship helps us take steps in the direction of faithfulness. As we recognize God's Inward Light present and speaking through all creation, the practice of watershed discipleship can help us understand what it means to participate in this Light-bearing community and how to begin our healing work.

Watershed discipleship has three main dimensions: 1) recognition of the watershed moment of ecological crisis in which we find ourselves, 2) being disciples *within* our geographical region or watershed, and 3) being disciples *of* the

---

28   Martin Kelley uses this updated version of the William Penn quote as the tagline to the QuakerQuaker website, http://quakerquaker.org.

other creatures and landscape elements around us in our watershed.[29]

You may be asking what a watershed is, so a watershed is the cradle or container in which we live, the area of land in which all water flows to a common location. At the top of a ridge, the water flows into one watershed or the other and eventually flows down into creeks, rivers, maybe lakes, and in most cases, eventually to the ocean. Permaculturist Brock Dolman calls this a basin of relations because all the creatures in the watershed rely on one another as a community, sharing the same water source and the life that grows because of that water.[30] So, we're in a watershed moment of ecological crisis, and this framework of watershed discipleship helps us

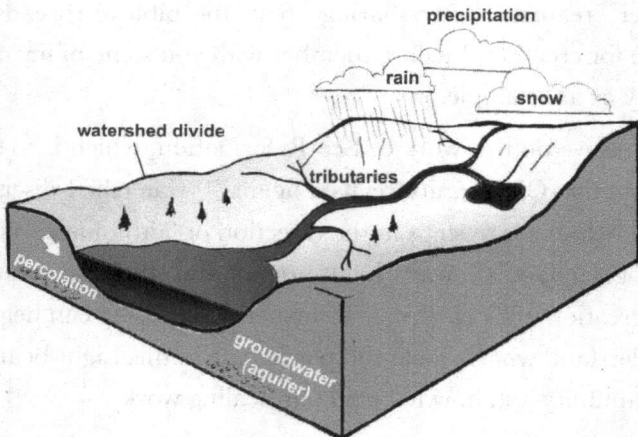

Watershed image is from the
NOAA Office for Coastal Management

29   Ched Myers, ed., *Watershed Discipleship: Reinhabiting Bioregional Faith and Practice* (Eugene, OR: Cascade Books, 2016).
30   Brock Dolman and Kate Lundquist, "Basins of Relations: A Citizen's Guide to Protecting and Restoring Our Watershed,"

think about a manageable size of our ecological community—it's not our work to fix everything, so it can sometimes feel overwhelming to know where to begin and where to end.

A watershed is also a nested concept, so in my case, I live in a small watershed with the folks that live around a local creek. That creek flows into the Willamette River, so the whole Willamette Valley is a larger watershed, including Eugene and Portland, and the Willamette flows into the Columbia River, which starts up in British Columbia, Canada, and flows down through Washington and then between Washington and Oregon. The Snake River is another major river that flows into the Columbia, and it starts on the edge of Wyoming and flows through Idaho—so most of the states of Oregon, Washington, Idaho, and part of the province of BC are part of the same watershed, the Columbia Basin. And then, of course, the Columbia flows into the Pacific Ocean, which connects us to all other watersheds.

Our watersheds can be a natural unit of care that we can imagine and work within, in partnership with and learning from the other people and species in our watershed. I love this rephrasing of the golden rule that eco-philosopher-poet Wendell Berry came up with: "Do unto others downstream what you would have those upstream do unto you."[31] Although many of our local environmental projects can become a little bit NIMBY-like,[32] watershed discipleship helps us imagine a portion of land about which we can particularly

---

third edition (Occidental, CA: Occidental Arts and Ecology Center Water Institute, 2018).

31 Wendell Berry, *Citizenship Papers* (Washington, DC: Shoemaker & Hoard, 2004), 135.

32 NIMBY is an acronym for "Not In My Back Yard."

care, and by caring for it, we are caring for the world. This, of course, only works if we aren't just outsourcing things that pollute and destroy ecosystems to other people's watersheds or that require unjust labor practices, so it requires us to build a mainly local economy. This is the "disciples within our watersheds" portion: we live within the community of all life in our watershed, and we collaborate with local groups and species to organize the care of our shared space.

To be disciples of our watersheds, we learn from the other creatures, landforms, and natural cycles in our region—we let them be our rabbi, our teacher. This is not simply a concept we created in recent decades, but it goes back to at least the fourth century. Augustine called creation the first book, and the Bible is the second book through which we can know God:

> Others, in order to find God, will read a book. Well, as a matter of fact there is a certain great big book, the book of created nature. Look carefully at it top and bottom, observe it, read it. God did not make letters of ink for you to recognize [God] in; [God] set before your eyes all these things [God] has made. Why look for a louder voice? Heaven and earth cries out to you, 'God made me.' ... Observe heaven and earth in a religious spirit.[33]

We can learn so much about God through observing

33 Augustine, "Sermon 68," in *The Works of St. Augustine, A Translation for the 21st Century: Sermons III* (51–94), ed. John E. Rotelle, transl. Edmund Hill (Brooklyn, NY: New City, 1991), 225.

the world around us. Probably many of you also feel like you connect with the Divine more easily when outside, looking at the stars, sitting by a river, breathing in the air of a forest, putting your hands in the soil of a garden, or simply feeling the warmth of sunlight on your face.

Being disciples in our watersheds means learning about the human and ecological history of our places, too, and learning how to become members of the community in our place. Therefore, a major piece of watershed discipleship is learning who lived on the land before and healing our relationship with the people and the land. Particularly for those of us who are descendants of European colonists, this requires enacting repentance in ways that work toward healing our watershed histories.[34] Many folks in the watershed discipleship community are learning, writing, and teaching about the Doctrine of Discovery, which I know you in NEYM have been learning about and wrote a minute repudiating some seven years ago, which is a great first step.[35] Healing the

---

34 Elaine Enns and Ched Myers, *Healing Haunted Histories: A Settler Discipleship of Decolonization* (Eugene, OR: Wipf & Stock, 2021).

35 See fn 3. The Doctrine of Discovery refers to a series of papal bulls from the fifteenth century, particularly *Dum Diversas* (1452), *Romanus Pontifex* (1454), and *Inter Caetera* (1493), in which the Catholic Church and European nations reinforced one another's justification for conquest of land, people, and natural resources. These documents authorize Christian nations to enslave Muslims and other people groups that are not Christian, claim *terra nullius* (or empty land) for European heads of state if that land is currently occupied by other-than-Christian groups, and forbid anyone to travel to lands newly "discovered" by Europeans to trade with, teach, or provide weapons or other tools to help the Indigenous people become strong enough to resist European dominance.

damage done by the Doctrine of Discovery is the current big work of watershed discipleship.

Those in the watershed discipleship community (as well as others who are working on this shift) talk about re-membering and reinhabiting. To re-member means to become a member again, to remember that you are part of a community. This includes recognizing (coming to know) and re-membering we participated in the harming of our planet, the harming of other people and creatures who live on it, which means we need to repent. The word "repent" literally means to turn around and go in a different direction. This is apt for the moment of ecological crisis we are in: we need to learn to go in the direction of reinhabiting our spaces in ways that are honoring to God and the rest of creation, rein-tegrating in ways that are participatory in the community of all life. Of course, when talking about "reconciling" with the Indigenous people of this land, it's difficult to reconcile when we have not exactly had conciliation before. There is much healing that needs to take place. Some Friends treat-ed Native Americans with more kindness than some other colonists, but our spiritual forebears still settled land taken in ways that were not just, participated in Indian boarding schools, and in other ways broke trust with Turtle Island's original inhabitants. Friends need to consider the story of the man Jesus healed with a second touch: our denomination perhaps "saw" in part but needed a second healing touch. I

For a more detailed treatment of the Doctrine of Discovery, Quaker culpability, and watershed discipleship, see: Cherice Bock, "Friends and Watershed Discipleship: reconciling with people and the land in light of the Doctrine of Discovery," *Quaker Religious Thought* 134 (Spring 2020): 35–46.

will return to a discussion of what this healing looks like for Friends later on, but first, I will describe watershed discipleship in more detail, particularly as it relates to the Bible.

Watershed discipleship is focused on themes found in the Bible, so I'll move into the second theme of this section. If you start looking for it, the land is really a character in the Bible, particularly in the Hebrew scriptures. Living in right relationship isn't just between people, God, and one another, but also includes the land: the full *oikumene* or global household of relations.[36]

In the first chapter of Genesis, God creates, separating the dry land and the water, and all of it is good, surrounding a tree of life. From that beginning, jump to the end, and notice that the final chapters of Revelation set out a vision of the new heaven and new earth, with a new Jerusalem whose central features are a river, a tree, and God's Light.[37] Through these bookends, the Bible offers us a vision of how to live in this *oikumene*, working together to co-create a beautiful and sustainable life.

As we journey through the Hebrew scriptures after the creation accounts, the land continues as a major part of the story.[38]

The books of the law teach the Israelites how to be a community before God, and although these laws would need to be

---

36 As described in section 2, *oikumene* refers to the global household, the Earth community.
37 Barbara Rossing, *The Rapture Exposed: The Message of Hope in the Book of Revelation* (New York, NY: Westview Press, 2004).
38 Ellen F. Davis, *Scripture, Culture, and Agriculture: An Agrarian Reading of the Bible* (New York, NY: Cambridge University Press, 2009).

updated by our standards, they are generally aimed toward caring for one another in a relatively just community. The land is a major player in the books of the law: it is to be cared for, and a marker of how well they are following the law is how healthy the land is. One of my favorite examples of this is Leviticus 20:22: God says, "You shall keep all my statutes and all my ordinances and observe them, so that the land to which I bring you to settle in may not vomit you out." Basically, if you're following the laws of God, the land will be healthy, but if you don't, the land itself will show you that you are not living within the covenant. It will become sick and vomit you out. As we are experiencing our lands and our weather events today signaling more and more inhospitable consequences for our collective actions, perhaps we can hear this as the voice of the land, vomiting us out for not living in ways that are faithful to the covenant.

Another important thing about the treatment of the land was that it was tied directly to the health and economic wellbeing of other people. Leviticus 19:9–10 states that they shouldn't harvest to the edge of the fields so that people could come glean—it says the "poor and the alien," in the NRSVue translation, meaning immigrants or foreigners.

The law points toward a *shalom* community, a community of care and resilience in which the economy, ecology, and society are interconnected in creative balance, much like what we are aiming toward when we talk about sustainability.[39] In sustainability conversations, the goal is to attend to

---

39 Randy Woodley, *Shalom and the Community of Creation: An Indigenous Vision,* Prophetic Christianity Series (Grand Rapids, MI: Eerdmans Publishing Co., 2012).

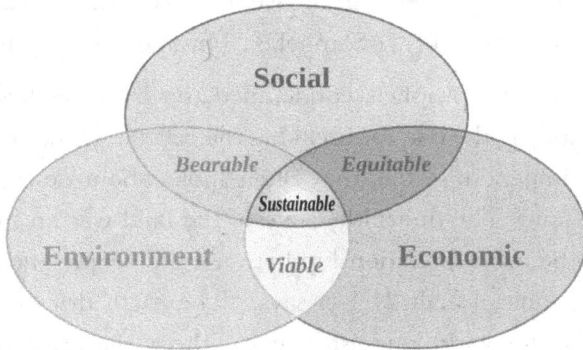

the triple bottom line where the social, economic, and eco-logical spheres are all maintained. In this way, life is bearable for people because they have their social and ecological needs met, life is just because everyone has enough resources to live off of, and life continues to be viable because those resources are only used in proportion to their ability to replenish. This is also the goal of the community described in the Jewish law.[40]

The Israelites finally get to inhabit the Promised Land after 400 years in a foreign land and forty years as nomads on wilderness land, but things don't really go well once they enter the land of milk and honey. Instead of focusing on God, they become comfortable in their new home, and they want to be like other nations: they want a king. They set up an empire. God warns them through Samuel that a king will force them into military conscription, force them to work his

---

40   Sustainability graphic from: Ian Overton, Matt Colloff, Michael Dunlop, Peter Wallbrink, and Geoffrey Michael Podger, "Nexus Webs: a Conceptual Framework for the Linkages and Trade-offs Between Water Use and Human Livelihood," *CSIRO*, Australia, December 2012. Reproduced with permission.

fields, confiscate their land to give it to his favored folks, and tax them unbearably (1 Samuel 8). This indeed happens.

When the prophets condemned the Israelites later for not following the law, for breaking the covenant, and warned of the impending exile, they often spoke about desecration of the land. The unhealthy state of the land was an indicator of the broken relationship between the people and God. For example, Isaiah 24:4–5 says, "The earth dries up and withers; the world languishes and withers; the heavens languish together with the earth. The earth lies polluted under its inhabitants, for they have transgressed laws, violated the statutes, broken the everlasting covenant." The health of the soil and the health of the human and other living species is inextricably linked.

The people of Israel are taken into exile because they have not been keeping the covenant, and in exile, they have to learn some challenging lessons. Jeremiah 29:4–7 says: "Thus says the Lord of hosts, the God of Israel, to all the exiles whom I have sent into exile from Jerusalem to Babylon: Build houses and live in them; plant gardens and eat what they produce. Take wives and have sons and daughters; take wives for your sons, and give your daughters in marriage, that they may bear sons and daughters; multiply there, and do not decrease. But seek the welfare of the city where I have sent you into exile, and pray to the Lord on its behalf, for in its welfare you will find your welfare." Even though they are not living in the Promised Land, they are to live in that land in ways that lead toward its prospering—not only in social terms but also by planting trees and gardens. This is the work of repentance, re-membering, and reinhabiting that I was talking about with watershed discipleship: they had to learn from their mistakes, repenting of their broken relationship with God, the land, and one another. They had to re-member who they were, and to do that, they had to become members of the community, even in exile, and learn how to really live as participants within God's covenant again.

We've already talked about Jesus in other sections, so I will skip ahead to the epistles and point out Romans 8, which has become one of the most often cited passages by ecotheologians, Romans 8:19–24. In this passage, the rest of creation is part of the story of reconciliation that God and humanity are engaged in. Creation is described as experiencing labor pains alongside us as we all work together to birth the new creation.

> 19 For the creation waits with eager longing for the revealing of the children of God, 20 for the creation was subjected to futility, not of its own will, but by the will of the one who subjected it, in hope 21 that the creation itself will be set free from its enslavement to decay and will obtain the freedom of the glory of the children of God. 22 We know that the whole creation has been groaning together as it suffers together the pains of labor, 23 and not only the creation, but we ourselves, who have the first fruits of the Spirit, groan inwardly while we wait for adoption, the redemption of our bodies. 24 For in hope we were saved. Now hope that is seen is not hope, for who hopes for what one already sees?

This passage has become beloved of ecotheologians

because it shows that it's not only humanity that is part of the story of God's work in the world but the entirety of creation. Theologians talk about "salvation history," meaning the story of how God is at work in salvific ways across time. We tend to think of this as humanity's story, but this passage shows all of creation is experiencing the story with us, bound up with us in the labor of co-creation.

To participate in this work of bringing forth the new creation is to participate in the story of salvation. The Greek word for salvation, *sozo*, is often used in contexts of healing: to save means to heal, to restore, and to be made well. In Greek, salvation is about bodily healing, and the passage in Romans 8 makes this clear when it talks about the "redemption of our bodies" and creation as a whole groaning, waiting with eager longing, for the renewal that will come with our enactment of the hoped-for future. When seen as an act of healing, salvation includes re-membering our history, repenting (turning around), and reinhabiting our appropriate place in the *oikumene*, the ecology of our planetary household.

White people in the United States have generally been taught *not* to remember: to be rootless and mobile, to be able to assimilate and become part of the same without particularity. As those who have displaced others and ourselves by colonization, those of us who are white have become disconnected from place and how we got here, from the impact of our actions, and from the lives of the creatures who nourish us. This makes it easy for us not to see the systems of oppression in which we are participating. For people of African descent or who are Indigenous to the lands now called the Americas, this un-remembering (or dis-membering) was forced, and the effects are the same—only more traumatic. Speaking as a white person, to re-member and reconnect is intensely counter-cultural because we benefit (in the short term) from a system of dominating others. We tell ourselves a story of benevolence and progress, of feeding the world and better educating people so they can have a higher standard of living. To re-member another story feels profoundly painful.

NEYM is already on this journey, and maybe others reading this are as well. I encourage you to continue this journey with authenticity. For those of us who are not Indigenous, we have to figure out how to reinhabit a place to which our ancestry does not belong, and we need much help in this work if we are going to do it faithfully and in a way that does not just continue to culturally appropriate.[41]

Part of the work of re-membering is, as we have already done, remembering our sacred stories, the biblical texts that help us understand how our tradition encourages us to belong to the land. Another part is re-membering our denominational history, and I think we're at a pivotal moment in Quaker history, where we're learning to see our own story through new lenses. It's good to be proud of our heritage, but we have often told ourselves overly-sanitized versions of our story. Donna McDaniel and Vanessa Julye, in *Fit for Freedom, Not for Friendship*, have given us a huge gift in critiquing the

---

41   During NEYM 2020 annual sessions, Friends approved taking "A Letter of Apology to Indigenous Peoples" back to their monthly meetings to discern whether and in what ways to offer this apology as a group, and how to go beyond apologies into action and right relationship. https://neym.org/working-group-right-relationship-indigenous-peoples

paternalism present in Quakers' abolitionism.[42] Similarly, Friends unpacking the history of William Penn in regard to slavery and purchase of the land of Pennsylvania, our role in Indian boarding schools, as well as the fact that we read out of meeting many of our most beloved historical Friends in their time—all of these critiques help us dismantle our own false vision of ourselves.

This requires a both/and perspective. We can see that earlier Friends were trying to do good, but they caused—or at least participated in—much harm. It is important for us to remember our ancestors and to love them. We can re-member our stories, not by sanitizing the parts we do not like but by telling ourselves the whole truth as we can discern it and learning from it in ways that lead to community healing.

I'll tell you a little bit of my own story as an example of re-membering. I grew up white in Oregon, and I really had no idea where my family came from, except that my last name was Eichenberger, and my mom's last name is Beebe, so we probably had some heritage in a German-speaking country and England. As I've started to re-member my own family story, I reflected on my mom's grandparents' family farm on the border of Oregon and Idaho, a place I visited several times with my cousins and grandpa, and I have many fond memories of hanging out with distant relatives and floating down irrigation ditches on inner tubes.

My great-grandparents, Fanny and Glen Beebe, were

---

42 Donna McDaniel and Vanessa Julye, *Fit for Freedom, Not for Friendship: Quakers, African Americans, and the Myth of Racial Justice* (Philadelphia, PA: Quaker Press of Friends General Conference, 2018).

the first to homestead that 240-acre plot starting in 1939. Civil engineers had built a series of dams and canals, opening up new areas to irrigation, utilizing the Homestead Act of 1862. The Northern Paiute and Western Shoshone had been expelled from this land in Eastern Oregon in the second half of the nineteenth century, but it had not been very usable for settlement due to its aridity. Now open to irrigation, this land was inexpensive to those who could show they had at least $2,000 in the bank, at least two years of successful farming experience, and who built a home on the land.[43] Glen and Fanny could meet these requirements, and they painstakingly cleared the land, disrupting the delicate high desert ecosystem, planting cash crops, and raising dairy cows.

In some ways, I look back in awe at my granny, who knew how to live off the land in ways that have not been passed down to me. In her letters, she talked about going out at dawn to shoot rabbits, then returning home to do all the household chores.[44] My mom remembers Granny going out back with an ax to butcher the Sunday chicken when my mom visited her grandparents as a kid. My grandpa talked about the shelves and shelves of canned food Granny put up each year, a skill I had to relearn from my mother-in-law and Internet videos.

Granny saw the hand of God at work in her family's

---

43 Timothy A. Dick, *The Vale Project, Research of Historic Reclamation Projects* (Denver, CO: Bureau of Reclamation History Program, 1993), 14–17.
44 My grandfather, Ralph Beebe, recorded some of his parents' correspondence in his 2015 self-published book, *The Ralph and Wanda Pierson Beebe Family*. This particular detail is from a letter she wrote in 1914. Ralph K. Beebe, *The Ralph and Wanda Pierson Beebe Family* (self-published, 2015), 1.

ability to get this homestead. She saw it as a blessing based on God's provision and her own and her husband's faithful work; a "bargain with God," she called it.[45] They experienced great hardship, and she often worried they would not have enough, but my grandpa remembers how Granny always set aside 10 percent of their net income for a tithe, no matter what, before paying any of their other bills. Additionally, they donated part of their land for the building of a Friends meetinghouse.[46] She sought to be a faithful woman. Still, knowing what I know about the damage to ecosystems and the destruction of the cultures of the Indigenous people groups that were forced to vacate that land, Granny's understanding of this land as a "blessing" for our family is problematic. Yet her story and heritage are part of mine.

Similarly, out in Newberg, where I live, Friend William Hobson chose this area as a location for a new Quaker community because, after visiting, he called it "a garden of the Lord."[47] It had a perfect climate, great soil, water access, and it was sparsely populated. (Most of the population of Kalapuya who had lived here had died of European diseases or had been forced onto reservations when Hobson arrived in the 1870s.)[48] Hobson convinced many Friends to move here, and I actually live on land that prominent local Friend,

45 Beebe, *Pierson Beebe Family*, 4.
46 Ridgeview Friends Church, built in 1941. Beebe, *Pierson Beebe Family*, 6.
47 Ralph K. Beebe, *A Garden of the Lord: A History of Oregon Yearly Meeting of Friends Church* (Newberg, OR: The Barclay Press, 1968), 28.
48 Harold Mackey, *The Kalapuyans: A Sourcebook on the Indians of the Willamette Valley*, second edition (Salem, OR: Mission Mill Museum Association and The Confederated Tribes of Grand Ronde, 2004).

Jesse Edwards, bought when he moved here 100 years before I was born. Edwards was born in Guilford, North Carolina, and moved to Oregon by way of Indiana. He was the second white man to own the land on which I live.[49]

He and a few others started Friends Pacific Academy in 1885, the school that became George Fox University (GFU). There was also an Indian boarding school twenty or so miles away near Forest Grove, Oregon, and the first principal of the school that became GFU had previously administered that Indian boarding school.[50] The land on which the university now sits was donated in the 1880s by the Deskins, who received the land as a Donation Land Claim after settling on it in 1846,[51] thirteen years prior to Oregon's statehood in 1859.[52] This was also prior to treaties with the Kalapuya

---

49 Beebe, *A Garden of the Lord.*
50 Henry J. Minthorn, first principal of Friends Pacific Academy, had been the superintendent of Chemawa Indian Boarding School. Ralph K. Beebe, *A Heritage to Honor, a Future to Fulfill: George Fox College, 1891–1991* (Newberg, OR: Barclay Press, 1991), 1–2. SuAnn M. Reddick, "Chemawa Indian School," *Oregon Encyclopedia, a project of the Oregon Historical Society,* January 20, 2021, https://www.oregonencyclopedia.org/articles/chemawa_indian_boarding_school/#.YG1LoeZlDOQ, accessed April 7, 2021.
51 The Deskins Donation Land Claim (DLC) is #54 in Township 3 South, Range 2 West of the Willamette Meridian in Yamhill County, Oregon. "Yamhill County Donation Land Claim and Certified Claim Numbers," Yamhill County website, McMinnville, OR, n.d., http://www.co.yamhill.or.us/surveyor/dlcs.htm.
52 Great Britain gave up its claim to the Oregon Territory to the United States in the Treaty of Washington in 1846, after the US Senate had claimed the region in 1843. Jean Barman, "Cascadia Once Upon a Time," in *Cascadia, the Elusive Utopia: Exploring the Spirit of the Pacific Northwest,* ed. Douglas Todd (Vancouver, BC: Ronsdale Press, 2008) 89–104.

and other local tribes in the 1850s.[53] These Friends were not directly related to me but are my spiritual forebears and the reason my family ended up here.

While preparing to give these talks to NEYM, I found out that I am a fifth-generation Newberg resident—and

---

53   The Stevens-Palmer Treaties were negotiated between representatives for the United States and the local tribes in 1854–1855, ceding 14 million acres to the United States from tribes in western Oregon and Washington. Earlier treaties with the Kalapuya and other regional tribes between 1850–1854 were not ratified. These promised Kalapuya reservations in the Willamette Valley, but the 1855 treaties (such as the Kalapuya Treaty signed in Dayton, OR) required tribes to confederate and move to areas such as the Warm Springs and Grand Ronde reservations. This brought on what is called Oregon's Trail of Tears in 1855–1856, where Indigenous people were forced to move onto reservations. Many of the treaty obligations on the part of the US government were not met: the tribes had negotiated to live on the reservations but to maintain grazing, hunting, and fishing rights, among other things. The treaty with the Confederated Tribes of Grand Ronde was nullified by the US government in 1954, but re-established in 1983. Sara L. Gonzalez, Ian Kretzler, and Briece Edwards, "Imagining Indigenous and Archaeological Futures: Building Capacity with the Confederated Tribes of Grand Ronde," *Archaeologies* 14, no. 1 (2018): 85–114, https://doi.org/10.1007/s11759-018-9335-0. Clark Hanson, "Oregon Voices: Indian Views of the Stevens-Palmer Treaties Today," *Oregon Historical Quarterly* 106, no. 3, *The Isaac I. Stevens and Joel Palmer Treaties, 1855–2005* (Fall, 2005): 475–489, https://www.jstor.org/stable/20615563. Melinda Jette, "Kalapuya Treaty of 1855," *Oregon Encyclopedia, a project of the Oregon Historical Society*, January 26, 2021, https://www.oregonencyclopedia.org/articles/kalapuya_treaty/#.YG3MUOZlDOQ, accessed April 7, 2021. "This IS Kalapuyan Land: Broken Treaties," Five Oaks Museum website, 2021, https://fiveoaksmuseum.org/this-is-kalapuyan-land-treaties-broken/, accessed April 7, 2021.

my children are the sixth generation.[54] That's pretty long around here, since the town was founded in 1891. My great-great-grandparents died here at Friendsview Retirement Community. I talked with my grandparents recently about my family history, and the most recent immigrants in my family moved from Switzerland in the 1840s. My grandpa can remember that his granddad, a second-generation US citizen, could pray in German, but that was the only recognizable cultural practice my grandpa remembers.

Several lines of my family go back farther than memory as Friends, having moved with the frontier across the country from North Carolina to Indiana, Iowa, and Kansas, to Idaho, to Oregon. Friends, including my family, benefited from the Doctrine of Discovery as they settled those lands across the United States, authorized by the state and blessed by the church. They could acquire land free or inexpensively simply by being white men (or married to white men).[55] Though this had the perhaps positive benefit of creating Quaker communities across the country that persist until this day, the land was only dubiously owned by the US government since treaties with Native American tribes had not been agreed upon, the land was not available equally to all people, and it contributed

---

54   Interview with Richard and Kathryn (Brandenburgh) Eichenberger, Friendsview Retirement Community, Newberg, OR, June 2020.

55   The Donation Land Claim Act of 1850 authorized white people and "American half-breed Indians" to claim 320 acres of land in Oregon Territory. Men could claim an additional 320 acres if married. Biracial Native Americans claiming land had to be US citizens (or be willing to become so), which meant they gave up their tribal rights and affiliations. "The Donation Land Claim Act (1850)," full text available at: https://pages.uoregon.edu/mjdennis/courses/hst469_donation.htm, accessed April 7, 2021.

to ecosystem destruction and species loss. While Friends did not create these policies, the Friends community was mostly white and took advantage of the readily accessible land they could homestead. Many times, they continued west because they had exhausted the land in just a few short years, using up the nutrient-rich topsoil that had taken centuries to develop.

Through re-membering my family history in this way, I am practicing watershed discipleship by reimagining my ancestral relationship with the land and its people and creatures: I am imbuing it with meaning that the people who lived it did not recognize, and I am noticing the wounds to people and creation that they left in their wake. Re-membering my family history is not just about learning the stories, but now it is about repentance—turning and going in another direction, and it is about reinhabiting—learning how to live here in a way that is respectful and helps heal the social and ecological rifts my people have created.

This work of watershed discipleship means reimagining not only the past but also the future, listening to the groaning of creation, and working alongside it to midwife in the new creation. Mennonites such as Elaine Enns, involved in articulating and enacting watershed discipleship, are participating in truth and reconciliation commissions in Canada between First Nations and Mennonites who immigrated due to religious persecution. Enns talks about having empathy for her ancestors, who experienced great trauma, and also recognizing that they inflicted trauma through receiving land that was not the Canadian government's to give.[56] This offers us a suggested pattern to follow. NEYM is engaging in work around

---

56   Enns and Myers, *Healing Haunted Histories*, 2021.

repentance and repair of relationships with local Indigenous folks, and this is something we're in the beginning stages of in the Sierra-Cascades Yearly Meeting as well.[57]

The work before us involves seeing clearly with that second spiritual healing touch: re-membering our stories and ourselves, so we can repent, turn around with a clear vision of the *shalom* community we want to help co-create. It means being disciples in our watersheds, caring for and tending the region in which we live for the sake of the whole planet, and partnering with others in our area. And it means being disciples of our watersheds, knowing that many of us are new here. We have a lot to learn: we can learn ancient wisdom about our Creator God even from our rock, tree, and river siblings with whom we share our watersheds.

---

57   For NEYM, see fn 39. SCYMF also approved a Minute of Right Relationship with Indigenous People in 2022. Equity & Inclusion Committee Report, Annual Sessions Minutes, Sierra-Cascades Yearly Meeting of Friends, May 2019, Canby, OR, https://www.scymfriends.org/minutes, accessed April 7, 2021.

4. "I Can't Breathe": *Ruach*, a Pandemic, and Environmental Justice

Take a deep breath in, and let it out. Breathe in and out.

Breathing exercises help us feel calmer and help us focus, help us endure pain. Breathing can help us transform our anger, recover from tears, be in touch with our bodies, and focus our prayers. We can survive weeks without food, days without water, but only minutes without breath.

This section is called: "'I Can't Breathe': *Ruach*, a Pandemic, and Environmental Justice," and while section 3 felt heavy, it also felt deep and true. Now is a moment to sit with that discomfort and let it deepen and expand within us, let it break us open—the cracks are where the Light gets in. This section is a lament and a challenge; it is uncomfortable and painful—and it is the work before us, Friends. The next section will be about hope, so hold that hope out before you and "Row On," my Friends. "Row On"; it is darkest before the dawn.[58]

In the Bible, the Spirit is associated with air, breath, and wind. The Hebrew word for Spirit is *Ruach*, and we can hear the breath sound in the word: *Ruach*. You have to breathe each sound; the word is an exhale. Try it: *Ruach*.

Ruach can mean air or wind, and it can even mean what we think of as the atmosphere. Although the ancient Hebrews didn't exactly have a conception of the atmosphere, they referred to atmospheric events such as thunderstorms

---

58   "Row On" was the theme for the 2020 NEYM Annual Sessions.

and changes in the climate during various seasons.[59] While we separate in our minds the atmosphere, the air, the wind, and our own breath, the Hebrews had one word for it: *ruach*. We breathe in the atmosphere. When we think of it this way, of course, our concerns about climate change and the green-house gas emissions that are changing our atmosphere impact us every time we fill our lungs.

Ruach can also mean Spirit. In Genesis 1:2, the Spirit of God—or the breath of God—hovers over the face of the water on the formless and void earth, and then there is light, and it is good, and there is evening, and there is morning: the planet begins to breathe.

God creates a person, an *A'dam*, out of the *adamah*, the soil of the land,[60] and God breathes God's Spirit into the clay person's nostrils—*Ruach*. And the person lives and is in the image of God. And there is evening, and there is morning, the Spirit's breath bringing life and rhythm to the planet.

And on the seventh day, God and creation rest, like taking a breath at the end of a long and fruitful week.

The breaths in and out, the evenings and the mornings, the rhythm of Sabbath at the end of each week—these are ways we participate in the life and the rhythms of God in this place. We're going to talk about these rhythms of breath and

---

59 Theodore Hiebert, "Air, the First Sacred Thing: The Conception of רוח in the Hebrew Scriptures," in *Exploring Ecological Hermeneutics*, eds. Norman C. Habel and Peter Trudinger, Symposium Series 48 (Atlanta, GA: Society for Biblical Literature, 2008), 9–19.

60 Davis, *Scripture, Culture, Agriculture*, 2008; Wilda C. Gafney, *Womanist Midrash: A Reintroduction to the Women of the Torah and the Throne* (Louisville, KY: Westminster John Knox Press, 2017).

Sabbath, these practices that connect us literally to the life of the Spirit and that connect us to one another as we share the atmosphere with all others on this planet. Breathe in, breathe out, and know that in all our distant places, we are sharing the breath of the Spirit.

But all is not right with our collective breath right now. We breathe in, and we breathe out in our separate spaces because the very air we breathe can make us sick and die due to the novel Coronavirus, COVID-19. In some places, we breathe in and out, and our lungs are ravaged by tiny particles that cause asthma and cancer and other diseases due to air pollution. In some places, we breathe in and out and choke due to wildfires burning the forests, the lungs of the Earth.

And all is not right with our air and our breath in ways that impact some people more than others. In the summer of 2020, we experienced amazing, prolonged protests over racial justice because of the death of a man—say his name: George Floyd—who died before our digital eyes, gasping for air under the knee of state-sanctioned violent authority, crying, "I can't breathe"—and he's not the first.[61] All is not right with our air and our breath when protesters who took

---

61 George Floyd, a Black man, died on May 25, 2020 in Minneapolis, MN, at the hands of a white police officer. Arrested for allegedly using a counterfeit $20 bill, he was not given the right to a fair trial, but was executed in the street under the officer's knee while bystanders attempted to stop the situation and took a video of the encounter. Other officers stood by and did not intervene. This nine-minute video sparked global racial justice protests. We had heard other victims say "I can't breathe" before, such as Eric Garner, Elijah McClain, and other people of color in the United States who have been killed as a result of law enforcement

to the streets in Portland, Oregon, and all over this country were maced, pepper-sprayed, and tear-gassed for claiming the Divine breath and image are present in Black bodies.

Mamas of all colors, shapes, and sizes wearing yellow shirts braved tear gas in solidarity with all the mamas who have lost babies, with all the Black people who have died at the hands of police brutality, and dads backed them up, blowing away the unholy air with leaf blowers strapped to their backs.[62] Rabbis showed up every single night in purple

---

encounters, but this time, it struck a chord with a broader swath of people.

62   As federal law enforcement agents escalated the situation of nightly direct actions at the Justice Center in Portland, OR, by kidnapping people in broad daylight and placing them in unmarked vans, a Wall of Moms formed for a time, with hundreds of Portland mothers showing up each night to form a barrier between police and other Black Lives Matter protesters. These moms responded to George Floyd calling out for his mama when he was being asphyxiated. The moms wore yellow shirts to identify themselves in hopes that their presence would draw attention to and shame the use of excessive force by federal agents. A group of dads also formed, many wearing orange. They brought leaf blowers, an ingenious way to blow clouds of tear gas back toward law enforcement officers. The Wall of Moms unfortunately fell apart quickly, as the founder of the group began to use her platform to elevate herself rather than to support the goals and wishes of Black Portlanders. A second group formed, Moms 4 Black Lives, led by Demetria Hester, a Black woman who had been attacked by Jeremy Christian in a famous and deadly incident on a MAX Light Rail train in 2017. Some moms continued to show up and wear yellow, but not in the numbers of the "Fed Wars," as protesters called these weeks in July 2020 just before I delivered this message to NEYM, roughly July 4–30, 2020. Wall of Moms members wore bike helmets and scuba goggles. Everyone wore regular masks due to the Coronavirus, and respirator or gas masks became protest equipment.

vests, enduring state-sponsored gassing to say, "No more, and never again, and never forget. *Ruach*."[63]

Breathe in, breathe out, Friends. All is not right with our air.

I've been out there sometimes in the streets, in my goggles and my helmet, with a yellow shirt or a purple clergy vest, breathing through a triple mask, protecting myself and others from COVID-19 and getting whiffs of tear gas. It's not about me. We center Black voices. But it is completely about me and my people, who have perpetuated racism and set up and benefited from systems of police violence. And it's not about me, but it is about me—my white body on the line, my privilege making the violence visible, my voice as Quaker "clergy," yelling at the top of my lungs, "This is what theology looks like!" with Presbyterians and witches and Indigenous and Methodists and Jews, and trying to heal the wounds my theology has previously inflicted. And it's not about me, but it is about me because this is our moment: the breath of the Spirit is flowing through our nation, and some are trying so hard to choke it, but we keep praying with our lungs and with our feet, *Ruach*.

And it's not about us as white folks, but it is about us—it's

---

63 A group of clergy called Portland Interfaith Clergy Resistance (PICR) regularly attended protests all summer and fall of 2020 (and beyond), wearing purple reflective vests. I began participating with them in July 2020 after going a few times as part of the Wall of Moms. As a Quaker, I do not usually call myself "clergy" in regular life, as that's not the way we speak of ourselves as Friends, but I am a recorded Friends minister. I will claim the clergy title when it allows me to show a visible sign of the faith community standing in solidarity with racial justice activists and because I get to participate in this network of fiercely loving interfaith leaders.

my white friend's college-age son going out to protest and my friend realizing it's the first time they've had to talk to their child about how to act when encountering the police. It's my thirteen-year-old son going to local demonstrations with me, asking questions and taking a stand, and later asking how to approach conversations with his friends about politics, race, and other injustices. It's about white folks speaking up for anti-racism in our small town's predominantly white school district, in solidarity with our students of color, and continuing to speak up until there is system change.[64]

It's not about white folks, but it is about us because one thing I didn't tell you in the previous section about my history was that my state, Oregon, was founded as whites only, authorizing officers to enforce the law, beating and then removing any Black people who tried to move here, and those officers trained a line of police that lead directly to those on the streets today. My great-grandparents could purchase a homestead because they had money in the bank and farming experience—and because they were white. My spouse and I could purchase a house partially because of an inheritance from my spouse's grandpa, who purchased his first home through the GI bill—benefits not given to African American soldiers.[65] And, though most of my Quaker ancestors were presumably

---

64 The school board of Newberg, OR, passed an anti-racism resolution in July 2020 with opposition from two school board members.

65 The Servicemen's Readjustment Act of 1944, commonly known as the GI Bill, helped white veterans attend college, purchase homes with very low mortgage interest rates, and offered unemployment benefits. "Servicemen's Readjustment Act of 1944," 78th Congress, 2nd Session, Ch. 268, June 22, 1944, 284–301, https://www.loc.gov/law/help/statutes-at-large/78th-congress/session-2/c78s2ch268.pdf, accessed April 7, 2021.

not overtly racist, my grandparents shared with me the story of my grandma's grandpa, who was "very Southern" and who "carried a pistol because of snakes, and because he worked with Black people."[66] This is my story, and this is our national story, whether we remember it or not.

"But what about the violence?" many say, by which they mean broken windows and graffiti, cardboard on fire, a shaken fence. They do not mean forcible removal across an ocean from one's people and land. They do not mean hundreds of years of enslavement or rape to produce more "property." They do not mean sheriff posses sent to bring back escaped slaves. They do not mean lynchings and Jim Crow laws. They do not mean red lines depicting where one cannot purchase a home. They do not mean the war on drugs, disproportionate school expulsion, or forced prison labor.

"But what about the violence?" many say, by which they mean tossed water bottles and broken glass. "What about Anti-fa?" as if there's something shameful about being anti-fascist. "What would we do without the police to keep us safe?" which is code for, "I care more about my property than the life-breath of Black human beings." Property destruction equated with Black lives says in an undercurrent: our society still views Black lives as property and values life in general for its economic worth. Crying "foul" at property destruction forgets who made the property laws and who those laws benefit.

This challenges us as Friends, doesn't it? Every day, I'm

66 Richard and Kathryn Eichenberger, interview with the author, Friendsview Retirement Community, Newberg, OR, June 17, 2020.

bumping up against my internalized white supremacy, even in my Quakerism, as I wish for "peaceful" protests, and I want the protesters to look "respectable." I find myself wanting folks to talk more nicely and to follow one leader—translation, I'm tone policing, trying to make myself and others comfortable and wishing for a hierarchy of authority. I'm discovering that it's not always clear who the Black leaders are who are respected by the community, and if you're not out there every night, it's hard to tell—if you don't have those relationships, it's easy to go along with the message of those who make you feel comfortable but who are not leading to system change.

When these thoughts and feelings arise in me, I breathe in the Spirit and out, in and out, and I replay the words of Dr. Martin Luther King, Jr. from his "Letter from Birmingham Jail," and I challenge myself and my white Quaker siblings not to just be the white moderate this time.

When a group of white Alabama clergymen issued "An Appeal for Law and Order and Common Sense,"[67] writing, "We do not believe that these days of new hope are days when extreme measures are justified in Birmingham,"[68] Dr. King responded, "Freedom is never voluntarily given by the oppressor."[69] He called white moderates out: "I had hoped that the

---

67 "Appendix 1: The White Ministers' Law and Order Statement, January 16, 1963," in *Blessed Are the Peacemakers: Martin Luther King, Jr., Eight White Religious Leaders, and the "Letter from Birmingham Jail,"* S. Jonathan Bass (Baton Rouge, LA: Louisiana State University Press, 2001), 233.

68 "Appendix 1," 236.

69 Martin Luther King, Jr., "Letter from Birmingham Jail," in *Blessed Are the Peacemakers: Martin Luther King, Jr., Eight White Religious Leaders, and the "Letter from Birmingham Jail,"* ed. S. Jonathan Bass (Baton Rouge, LA: Louisiana State University Press, 2001), 242.

white moderate would understand that law and order exist for the purpose of establishing justice, and that when they fail to do this they become dangerously structured dams that block the flow of social progress."[70]

Rather than being a moderate, King entreats us to be extremists: "Was not Jesus an extremist in love...? ... So the question is not whether we will be extremist but what kind of extremist we will be. Will we be extremists for hate or will we be extremists for love?"[71]

Dr. King's breath was cut short too soon, but he was already using it to draw the connections between racism and imperialism and violence, the war in Vietnam, the economy, and environmental concerns. In the same "Letter from Birmingham Jail," he said, "I am cognizant of the interrelatedness of all communities.... Injustice anywhere is a threat to justice everywhere. We are caught in an inescapable network of mutuality, tied in a single garment of destiny. Whatever affects one directly affects all indirectly."[72] We've known about the interrelatedness of race and economy and violence and the environment since the 1960s.

And as Friends, we've known about it even longer through our own prophet, John Woolman, born 300 years ago. He noted the evils of slavery, as we probably all know, and he also expressed concern over many parts of the economic system that were controlled by imperialism, unjust labor practices, animal abuse, industrial pollution, and excessive wealth. He wrote, "The produce of the earth is a gift from our gracious

---

70 King, "Letter from Birmingham Jail," 246.
71 Ibid, 250.
72 Ibid, 239.

78

Creator to the inhabitants, and to impoverish the earth now to Support outward greatness appears to be an injury to the succeeding age."[73]

Woolman did not compromise his principles, choosing to walk instead of riding a horse, deciding to stop being a shop-keeper because he did not want to amass too much wealth, and wearing undyed clothes to protest slavery. The famous quote from Woolman is still convicting today: "May we look upon our treasures, the furniture of our houses, and our garments, and try whether the seeds of war have nourishment in these our possessions."[74] Woolman was an "extremist for love," following the Spirit courageously until his last breath.

Through him, Friends have known about the intercon-nectedness between race, oppression, economy, land confisca-tion, ecology, and war for three centuries, but as a Religious Society of Friends, we have not collectively followed through on actions that would interrupt the systems of oppression Woolman noticed.

Racial justice and state-authorized violence are the focus of the protests at the moment, rightly saying no to those chok-ing the life-breath out of Black Americans through systems of policing designed to support the status quo. But this is only one part of a set of interconnected issues.

---

73 John Woolman, "Conversations on the True Harmony of Mankind & How It May Be Promoted," in *John Woolman and the Affairs of Truth: The Journalist's Essays, Epistles, and Ephemera*, ed. James Proud (San Francisco: Inner Light Books, 2010), 169.

74 John Woolman, "A Plea for the Poor," in *The Journal of John Woolman and "A Plea for the Poor,"* ed. John Greenleaf Whittier (Eugene, OR: Wipf & Stock Publishers, 1998 [1871, 1774]), 241.

We're also in the midst of a global pandemic, in case you hadn't noticed, and COVID-19 is a disease that makes it difficult for people to breathe. And it is disproportionately infecting and killing people of color in our country. A UCLA study released in late July 2020 shows Black and Latinx Americans are twice as likely to die of this Coronavirus in Los Angeles and New York City than other residents.[75] Level of income is a compounding factor, but race is more strongly correlated. Why? There are economic factors relating to the race of those considered "essential workers" in this moment, who do not have the privilege of working from home. Folks of color are exposed to more possibilities of catching the virus. These jobs often receive low wages, so larger groups of people—intergenerational families—often share the same living space.

There are also environmental factors: those with underlying health conditions, such as asthma, cardiovascular diseases, and cancer are at more risk if they catch this Coronavirus, and these public health concerns are directly related to the air quality and presence of other toxins in one's neighborhood. Research for the last fifty years shows a consistent correlation between the siting of toxic waste and other polluting facilities near communities of color, where race is a stronger predictor than economic status. This is environmental racism, and the advocacy and activism to alleviate this problem are called environmental justice.

---

75   Laura E. Marinez, et al., COVID-19 in *Vulnerable Communities: an Examination by Race/Ethnicity in Los Angeles and New York City* (Los Angeles, CA: University of California Los Angeles Latino Policy & Politics Initiative, Center for the Study of Latino Health and Culture, July 27, 2021), https://ph.ucla.edu/sites/default/files/attachments/LPPI-LA-v-NY-Report.pdf.

Back in the 1970s, Robert Bullard researched the siting of landfills near communities of color, and the landmark "Toxic Wastes and Race in the United States," sponsored by the United Church of Christ, came out in 1987, showing the correlation between factories producing hazardous waste and the storage of toxic waste (or brownfields), and communities of color.[76] In 2007, the UCC and Bullard performed a follow-up, "Toxic Wastes and Race at Twenty," which found the same problems still exist—and even that "people of color are found to be *more* concentrated around hazardous waste facilities than previously shown."[77] Though George Floyd couldn't breathe in the moment because he had a literal knee on his neck, communities of color are living with the empire's knee on their necks every day, causing disproportionate rates of cardiovascular diseases, asthma, and cancer—and directly relating to their risk of lethal COVID-19.

While climate change will adversely affect all of us at some point—and as I gave these talks, New England experienced tropical storm Isaias—our collective climate impacts are disproportionately affecting folks of color in the US already. This is not even to mention the disproportionate impact on people in other countries. Much of the most important and inspiring work to address the global climate justice movement

76   Robert D. Bullard, et al., *Toxic wastes and race in the United States: a national report on the racial and socio-economic character-istics of communities with hazardous waste sites* (New York, NY: United Church of Christ Commission for Racial Justice, 1987).

77   Robert D. Bullard, et al., *Toxic Wastes and Race at Twenty, 1987–2007: A Report Prepared for the United Church of Christ Justice & Witness Ministries* (Cleveland, OH: United Church of Christ Justice & Witness Ministries, 2007).

is happening in the poorest and most impacted countries, as Indigenous folks and those most vulnerable to flood, drought, and severe storms speak prophetically to the rest of the world.

The links between this pandemic and other recent epidemics (such as Ebola outbreaks) and our interaction with the rest of creation are clear: these new viruses come into contact with human beings because we encroach on habitat where we do not belong. This also links with our economic system: when food is scarce, people hunt and eat food they would not otherwise eat or look for exotic species to sell. Our global economy is so intertwined that viruses easily travel the planet, carried far beyond their usual reach due to international trade.

So, *Ruach*, help us, this is huge, and it can start to feel overwhelming. Take a deep breath—feel the Spirit moving in and out of your lungs. Feel the breath of God connecting you to all other life on this planet. Re-member.

Part of opening ourselves up to the Divine Light discussed in section 2 is that it exposes things we try to keep hidden, things we've tried to ignore. Take another breath, and allow the Spirit's courage to build you up.

In the previous section, we talked about the need for repentance. Rather than going the direction we've been going, focusing only on what benefits us and our own species or people group, attempting to dominate and control all others, we can go in a different direction: a direction that tends toward healing, collaborating with our communities for mutual healing. How do we get there?

If we are repenting, that means we've done something

wrong: we have sinned. I know "sin" is not a really popular term among many of us right now, but I think we need to call it what it is and open up our understanding of sin.

Sin has been conceived in the United States context as an individual matter, and the remedy is personal confession and repentance in order to earn forgiveness and salvation in the form of eternal life. While I do think personal responsibility and repentance are important, and I'm not arguing against eternal life, I want to reorient our understanding of what "sin" means.

The term for sin, *hamartia*, has two main meanings: one is flagrantly sinning in ways that intentionally cause harm, and the other has to do with missing the mark. We could say that one is intentional and mean-spirited, while the other is passively participating in something sinful. A sin is something that focuses on self rather than faithfulness—a focus on ego rather than eco. This is not to say that we have to be self-sacrificing martyrs, ignoring our own needs, but instead, it means our healing is bound up in our actions of care for and with the other people and species in our community.

We can sin actively, or we can sin passively. I assume most of us are nice people who don't generally go around actively harming others. But this does not let us off the hook. More insidious is collective sin, which is what I'm talking about when I say "sin we engage in passively." The systems and structures of power, the *kosmos* I pointed out in section 2, are the ways we participate in collective sin.[78]

---

78 Learn more about collective sin in: Cynthia Moe-Lobeda, *Resisting Structural Evil: Love as Ecological-Economic Vocation* (Minneapolis, MN: Fortress Press, 2013).

This type of sin oppresses some while others benefit. Those of us who live in the United States benefit from the ways our military acts around the world, and though we do not engage in violence ourselves, we experience the benefits that come from it. We do not destroy forests in order to grow palm trees ourselves, but we participate when we purchase products using palm oil.[79] We don't personally frack natural gas, we don't personally build oil and gas pipelines, we don't personally operate coal plants, and we don't personally remove mountaintops, but when we use fossil fuels, we passively participate in these systems, and I posit that these actions are collective sin. We didn't personally enslave people or take land from Native Americans, but we still live here, and those injustices have not been resolved. These are just a few examples of collective sin.

Ecotheologian Cynthia Moe-Lobeda puts it this way: "Sin in its fullest sense refers to disorientation from right relationship with God, which then leads to disorientation from right relationship with self, others, and all of creation."[80] We participate in this collective sin by living within the structures of our society that cause harm to other people and other creatures, and we generally try to ignore that this is what

---

79 E.g., C. Nellemann, et al., *The Last Stand of the Orangutan: State of Emergency: Illegal Logging, Fire and Palm Oil in Indonesia's National Parks* (Norway: United Nations Environment Programme, Great Ape Survival Partnership, GRID-Ardenal, 2007); Varshay Vijay, et al., "The Impacts of Oil Palm on Recent Deforestation and Biodiversity Loss," *PLoS ONE* 11, no. 7 (2016): e0159668, DOI: 10.1371/journal.pone.0159668.
80 Moe-Lobeda, *Resisting Structural Evil: Love as Ecological-Economic Vocation*, 58.

we are doing, engaging in what Moe-Lobeda calls "moral oblivion."[81]

This condition is called "affluenza": "A painful, contagious, socially transmitted condition of overload, debt, anxiety, and waste resulting from the dogged pursuit of more."[82] Why do we pursue more? Because our system is set up in such a way that if we don't constantly pursue more, if we don't try to dominate at every turn, we will be one of the oppressed.

The message that flows through the biblical witness is liberation from this fear, so we do not have to participate in collective sin. And the biblical message is an utterly economic message, as well as a spiritual, social, and ecological one. When the rich man asks Jesus what he must do to be saved, what does Jesus say? He says, "Sell what you own, and give the money to the poor" (Mark 10:21; Luke 18:22). Jesus' message is absolutely about property, but it's about shared property and supporting one another, and absolutely not about protecting property from others. When Jesus clears the Temple in a passage that makes many Friends skittish, this is absolutely about economy and property and the complete incompatibility of a predatory economy within Jesus' religion (Matthew 21; Mark 11; Luke 19). Jesus says they've made the Temple a "den of thieves," they are setting up religious expectations that disadvantage the poor, and he is having none of it.

When Jesus lays out his mission in Luke 4:18–19, he says, "The Spirit of the Lord is upon me, because he has anointed

---

81 Moe-Lobeda, *Resisting Structural Evil: Love as Ecological-Economic Vocation*, 90.

82 John de Graff, David Wann, Thomas H. Nayler, *Affluenza: The All-Consuming Epidemic* (San Francisco, CA: Berrett-Koehler Publishers, Inc., 2005), 2.

me to bring good news to the poor. He has sent me to proclaim release to the captives and recovery of sight to the blind, to set free those who are oppressed, to proclaim the year of the Lord's favor." God's breath is in his lungs, and his message is good news—for whom? For the poor and those ostracized by their communities. He proclaims the year of the Lord's favor—the Year of Jubilee, the Sabbath of Sabbaths (Leviticus 25), and this message of economic and holistic liberation led directly to his lynching at the hands of the empire.

To bring us back to the Spirit's rhythms, the breathing in and out, in and out, participating in the ebb and flow of God's good creation, I'm going to end by talking about the practice of Sabbath as an act of liberation. When we practice the Sabbath for humanity, we create a communal model that counteracts our ability to set up systems of collective sin.

The Sabbath is a weekly day off in which every person gets to rest—the privilege of rest isn't dependent on one's economic status. Even animals get to rest.[83] Compare this to the United States; not everyone can afford to take a day off.

The Sabbath was not only once a week but also one year out of every seven when the fields were given a rest (e.g., Exodus 23:10–12, Leviticus 25). This was a Sabbath rest for the land as well as the workers. Rather than trying to squeeze out every last productive ounce from a piece of land, this method respected the rhythms of the land and required everyone to work together to stock up for lean years.

---

83   Exodus 20:8–11, 23:10–12; Leviticus 25:2–7; Deuteronomy
     5:12–15. See: A. Rahel Schafer, "Nonhuman Sabbath
     Repose in Pentateuchal Law," *Bulletin for Biblical Research* 23,
     no. 2 (2013): 167–186.

There was also a special Sabbath year, one year every seven-times-seventh year—the Year of Jubilee in which a complete reset of the economy was to occur. Debts were forgiven, and people returned to their ancestral land (e.g., Deuteronomy 15:1–18). The whole economy was to be set up to account for this Year of Jubilee and to make it fair, so the wealth gap was limited. Can you imagine how freeing it would be to live in a society that operated in this way? The implications of Sabbath-following are that we care about the wellbeing of the whole community and that we recognize that our wellbeing is bound up in the health and safety of others.

Rather than a race war in which we must try to choke one another so we have enough to breathe, living within the Spirit's rhythms allows us all to breathe in the fresh air and to rest without fear. We recognize that our healing is bound up in one another's stories, in one another's flourishing.

At Civil Rights Movement icon and Representative John Lewis's funeral, Bernice King prayed that God would grant us each a double portion of Lewis's courage and moral fortitude. She closed her prayer with: "We will continue to get into good trouble as long as you grant us the breath to do so."[84]

May it be so.

---

84 Bernice King, "Dr. Bernice King speaks at John Lewis' funeral," ABC News, July 30, 2020, https://youtu.be/Bj3OXvM-1Jg.

5. A Quaker Ecology: Our Bodies as Fractals of Hope

In the first four sections of this booklet, we've been through some serious work, taking a look at our histories and our stories about ourselves, noticing the ways we've contributed to and internalized white supremacy and settler colonialism despite our best intentions, and we've faced into the harm we've caused. We've cast a vision for the Eco-Reformation we want to see in our denomination and in our world, and we've found meaning and purpose in the sacred text handed down to us, the stories of people of faith who have come before. We've reimagined our own tradition's theology of the Inward Light, transforming it into an ecotheology of Light that connects us all as participants in the community of all life, and we've imagined a unit of care in which we can partner with others in our regions to learn how to do the work of watershed discipleship. Now, we're turning the corner toward hope, which is both a vision of a hoped-for future as well as the state we're in while we're working to reach that future.

And how do we do this work of hoping? We engage in hoping as embodied beings. Hope happens when we're realistically aware of our present reality, grounded in an understanding of our past successes and failures, have a vision of what we're working toward, and are taking steps to get there.[85] All of this happens through our bodies and through the meaning we make of our past, present, and future.

---

85   See a more complete treatment of hope and its relationship to ecotheology in: Cherice Bock, "Climatologists, Theologians, & Prophets: Toward an Ecotheology of Critical

Perhaps most importantly, hope happens best when in the context of a community that can hold our hope for us when we're feeling hopeless and that can keep taking steps toward what we hope for together, even when the outcome we hope for feels impossible.[86] In this final section, we will consider the topic, "A Quaker Ecology: Our Bodies as Fractals of Hope." There are at least three things in that title that need explaining: 1) bodies, 2) fractals, and 3) imagining how this way of hoping relates to a Quaker ecology.

We'll start with talking about bodies. I'm going to use this metaphor about bodies to help us imagine who we are in the world and how we can move within and toward the Eco-Reformation we want to see.

When I took an ecology class, my concept of my self and identity changed. I had previously thought of myself as an individual, as many of us probably do. I'm me, myself, and I: I'm my consciousness and my subconscious, my spirit and soul, and my body, journeying forward through time.

But in ecology, we started talking about ecosystems and biomes and landscapes and communities, and I realized that while I am an individual, I am also many other things, and whether I can call myself an individual "organism" is questionable.[87] First, I'm made up of a lot of other organisms: there are all kinds of different gut flora present in my body, without

Hope," *Cross Currents* 66, no. 1 (March 2016): 8–34, DOI: 10.1111/cros.12171.

86 Victoria McGeer, "The Art of Good Hope," *The Annals of the American Academy of Political and Social Science* 592, no. 1 (2004): 100–127.

87 T. F. H. Allen and Thomas W. Hoekstra, *Toward a Unified Ecology: Complexity in Ecological Systems* (New York, NY: Columbia University Press, 1992).

which I couldn't process food or fight off invading viruses and bacteria. These microorganisms that help me can't survive very well on their own outside a human body (or, in some cases, other animal bodies); I'm their habitat, and they make up communities, populations, and ecosystems within my body.[88] All the ecosystems in my body form a biome. On the outside of my body, my skin is a landscape, and plenty of little microscopic critters live on my skin. Maybe that sounds gross, but it's also amazing! So am I an individual organism? Scientists estimate that perhaps 90 percent of the cells in our bodies are bacteria—around 40,000 species—and without them, our bodies wouldn't function.[89] Do all those other tiny creatures count as parts of me, or are they individuals themselves? Together, do we form a community in and on my own body?

Going the other direction, I am one human being, but humans are social animals; we can't actually survive by ourselves. We need someone to raise us, and then we need someone to help us reproduce, so our species has to be at least somewhat social. I'm a member of a population of my species or perhaps a colony. Some living entities share properties of organisms and colonies because part of the colony can break off and form a new colony. This is kind of like us: we can't really exist alone, but we can break off in a group and form another group. Are we individual organisms, or are we necessarily one part of a colony?

---

88 Cynthia L. Sears, "A dynamic partnership: Celebrating our gut flora," *Anaerobe* 11, no. 5 (2005): 247–251, DOI: 10.1016/j.anaerobe.2005.05.001.

89 Daniel N. Frank and Norman R. Pace, "Gastrointestinal microbiology enters the metagenomics era," *Current Opinion in Gastroenterology* 24, no. 1 (January 2008): 4–10, DOI: 10.1097/MOG.0b013e3282f2b0e8.

Also, while human beings need other people to survive, we cannot survive without relying on other species as food and shelter. We're not only part of a colony (a group of human beings who directly rely on each other) and a population (all human beings in our ecosystem), but we're also part of a community: those beings of different species who work together and react together to one another and their landscape factors, the whole of which is greater than the sum of its parts. A community is something more than just a collection of individuals because they accommodate one another and rely on one another. As human beings, we're part of a community because we need other species in order to survive.

Additionally, we are part of an ecosystem, and we need that in order to survive: an ecosystem is the way that nutrients are cycled through a landscape and its various species and communities: the air, water, soil, and light, and how the various species interact through a web of relations to make use of the energy and nutrients in these elements to nourish one another. Without the nutrients that other species transform into usable forms, we would not get all the nourishment we need, so we are completely dependent on the continuation of our ecosystem functions. For example, human beings do not efficiently transform the energy the planet receives from the sun into nutrients our bodies can use, so we rely on plants to do much of that work, and different plants do different parts of that work. As was referred to earlier in the booklet, trees are connected by underground fungal networks called mycelia, connecting through mycorrhizae to the roots of trees. These fungal networks transfer different types of nutrients between different species of trees so that a tree may specialize in one way of photosynthesizing and receive other types of nutrients from other trees that specialize in other energy transformations.[90]

I could go on and on with the amazing ways that ecosystems cycle nutrients so that each species receives what it needs and contributes what it can, but I think you get the point—all the entities in the ecosystem help one another by doing things none of the others in that ecosystem can do and without which the other species would not be as healthy—so is the ecosystem a collection of individuals, or is it in itself a sort of body?

Of course, none of us would be able to exist without a hospitable planet (or a really sophisticated spaceship—but even that would need a healthy planet to get it started).[91] We need all the ecosystems forming together into land and ocean biomes and into one big biosphere at the right distance from a star's energy in order for all the systems, processes, and relationships to work together so that we can continue to live and breathe and have clean water. The planet is a body, or perhaps the solar system, holding us in a gravitational place as we spin through the universe.

All of these are different scales of bodies: the microorganisms inside my body, myself as an individual organism, the population, the community, the ecosystem, each biome, and the whole planetary biosphere. In a very real way, each

90   Peter Wohlleben, *The Hidden Life of Trees: What They Feel, How They Communicate, Discoveries from a Secret World*, transl. Jane Billinghurst, first English edition (Berkeley, CA: Greystone Books, 2016).
91   Kenneth Boulding, "The Economics of the Coming Spaceship Earth," in *Environmental Quality in a Growing Economy*, ed. Henry Jarrett (Baltimore, MD: Resources for the Future/John Hopkins University Press, 1966).

of these could be described as an individual or as a community—each of them could be described as a body or as a collection of bodies.

This is where part 2 comes in: fractals. According to mathematician Benoit Mandelbrot, "A fractal is a shape made of parts similar to the whole in some way."[92] Fractals appear the same or similar at different levels or scales. They exhibit similar patterns. Some call this "expanding symmetry" or "unfolding symmetry." My thought is that a body is a type of fractal that has both individual and communal characteristics and can be found at different scales.

Some examples of fractals are mathematical and precise such as these triangles, snowflakes, or squares. Then there's the somewhat famous Mandelbrot set, which is a visualization of an equation having to do with the square root of negative 1,[93] and it creates a cardioid image with a circle. Then,

---

92   Benoit B. Mandelbrot, "Self-affine fractal sets," in *Fractals in Physics: Proceedings of the Sixth Trieste International Symposium on Fractals in Physics*, ICTP, Trieste, Italy July 9–12, 1985, eds. L. Pietronero and E. Tosatti (North-Holland, Amsterdam: Elsevier, 1986), 3–15.

93   The Mandelbrot set is a mathematical equation graphed two dimensionally—where the x-axis is the one-dimensional number line and the y-axis is positive and negative imaginary numbers. The points on the graph that are part of the Mandelbrot set are ascertained by the equation $z = z^2 + c$. The numbers within the set stay within a bounded area, while the numbers that are not part of the set continue toward infinity. A pattern of a cardioid shape with an appended bulb shape is formed, and at smaller and larger scales, similar patterns can be seen as one performs the equation with smaller and smaller increments. Robert L. Devaney, "The Mandelbrot Set, the Farey Tree, and the Fibonacci Sequence," *The American Mathematical Monthly* 106, no. 4 (1999): 289–302, DOI:10.2307/2589552.

around the edges are similar shapes, and around the edges of that are similar shapes. You can keep zooming in, and you see similar patterns emerging at every scale—some of them spirals and others this cardioid with a circle. It goes on forever and ever, as far as we can compute, at smaller and smaller scales and at larger and larger scales. The theoretical outline of this shape would be infinite.

In the case of all these mathematical fractals, they look similar at various scales. In the Mandelbrot set, they don't look the same at every iteration or scale, but they share similarities of shape and pattern. Fractals also exist in the natural world, and some represent mathematical concepts: the nautilus shell is the expression of the Fibonacci sequence.[94] And you've got fractals that are natural patterns, like the explosion—anywhere that you see a significant enough impact, from a splattered raindrop to a crater from a meteorite. The branch pattern can be seen from our veins to trees to rivers.[95]

The point here is that a fractal is a pattern that shares similarities across different scales, and fractals exist as mathematical concepts as well as natural patterns.

So I'm thinking of our bodies as fractals in which we experience embodiment at various scales. I am a body that houses a community. I am also part of human bodies at various scales: in the faith community, I'm part of the bodies of my own congregation, my yearly meeting, the wider body of

---

94 Fibonacci Sequence: each number is the sum of the two preceding numbers, $1 + 1 = 2$, $1 + 2 = 3$, $2 + 3 = 5$, $3 + 5 = 8$, and so forth. When graphed, this forms a spiral line. Devaney, "The Mandelbrot Set, the Farey Tree, and the Fibonacci Sequence," 300–301.

95 Allen and Hoekstra, *Toward a Unified Ecology*, 67.

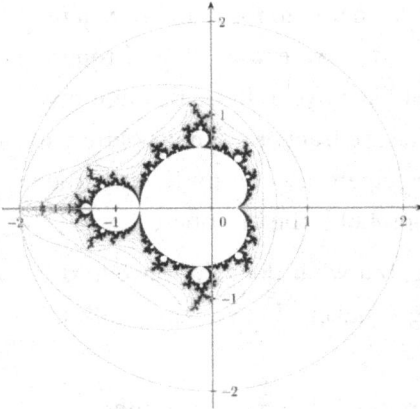

Geek3, "Plot of the Mandelbrot Set,"
Creative Commons BY-SA 3.0, 2009.

Fifth iteration of the half-square fractal,
creative commons license.

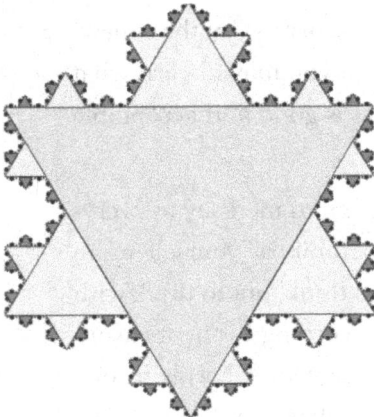

Jim Belk, "Koch Snowflake Triangles,"
public domain, 2007.

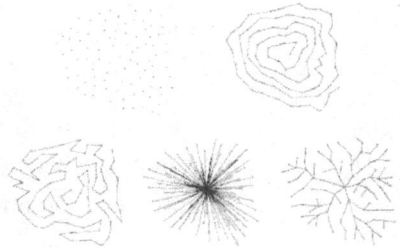

Patterns found in nature.

Friends. The populations of human beings in my town and region also function as a body politic. I participate as part of a body with the other species that form a community and the species and inputs that cycle energy to form an ecosystem in my region. The nutrients in the waterways flow through the body of my ecosystem just like oxygen flows through my veins, and waterways and veins are fractals—similar patterns on a different scale. We participate as one body with the whole *oikumene*: the global household, the biosphere.

That's nice, you're saying, but what does this have to do with the Bible or with being Quaker? Let's take a look at Romans 12.

> 1 I appeal to you therefore, siblings, by the mercies of God, to present your bodies as a living sacrifice, holy and acceptable to God, which is your spiritual worship. 2 Do not be conformed to this world, but be transformed by the renewing of your minds, so that you may discern what is the will of God—what is good and acceptable and perfect.
>
> 3 For by the grace given to me I say to everyone among you not to think of yourself more highly than you ought to think, but to think with sober judgment, each according to the measure of faith that God has assigned. 4 For as in one body we have many members, and not all the members have the same function, 5 so we, who are many, are one body in Christ, and individually we are members one of another. 6 We have gifts that differ according to the grace given to

us: prophecy, in proportion to faith; 7 ministry, in ministering; the teacher, in teaching; 8 the exhorter, in exhortation; the giver, in generosity; the leader, in diligence; the compassionate, in cheerfulness.

9 Let love be genuine; hate what is evil, hold fast to what is good; 10 love one another with mutual affection; outdo one another in showing honor. 11 Do not lag in zeal, be ardent in spirit, serve the Lord. 12 Rejoice in hope, be patient in suffering, persevere in prayer. 13 Contribute to the needs of the saints; extend hospitality to strangers.

14 Bless those who persecute you; bless and do not curse them. 15 Rejoice with those who rejoice, weep with those who weep. 16 Live in harmony with one another; do not be haughty, but associate with the lowly; do not claim to be wiser than you are. 17 Do not repay anyone evil for evil, but take thought for what is noble in the sight of all. 18 If it is possible, so far as it depends on you, live peaceably with all. 19 Beloved, never avenge yourselves, but leave room for the wrath of God; for it is written, "Vengeance is mine, I will repay, says the Lord." 20 No, "if your enemies are hungry, feed them; if they are thirsty, give them something to drink; for by doing this you will heap burning coals on their heads." 21 Do not be overcome by evil, but overcome evil with good.

In this chapter, the first two verses are about us as individual bodies. We're asked to present our bodies to God, and this is our spiritual act of worship. Our bodies are the location in which we encounter God and can be transformed. In another place, our bodies are called the Temple of the Holy Spirit (1 Corinthians 6:19), which makes sense with our understanding of the Inward Light. By worshiping God with our bodies and our whole selves, we are able to discern God's will so that we can *not* be conformed to the patterns of this world, the patterns that try to control and dominate. Instead, we participate in the transformation that God is effecting in the world.

Then, in verses 3–8, Paul uses the metaphor of the body of Christ to refer to our faith communities. We are the body of Christ: together, we are the embodiment of God in the world because God chooses to work through our bodies individually and as a collective. The body of Christ exists at various scales, from our individual bodies to our meeting, to our yearly meeting, to the Society of Friends, all the way up to the church universal across time and space. Romans 8:19–24 shows us that even the whole creation is part of this body, groaning in labor pangs, birthing the new creation, and bound up in the salvation process with us—and Paul specifically mentions the redemption of our bodies. Our bodies are the location in which we encounter God and the location in which salvation happens. I'll mention again that the word for salvation in Greek (*sozo*) is about healing and wellness, so it relates to this idea of our bodies as an important metaphor for understanding this Eco-Reformation.

Romans 12:1–2 is about our individual bodies, verses 3–8

are about the body of Christ, which we make up as a group, and then verses 9–21 tell us how we relate to one another, mostly dealing with relationships within the body of Christ. We're to love and serve, be patient and persevere, rejoice, show hospitality, and meet each other's needs. We're to bless others and always want what's best for them, living in harmony. We're to show empathy, feeling with one another in both positive and negative emotional states.

Some scholars think verses 17–21 refer to relationships with those outside the congregation, or, at least, they clearly refer to situations of conflict in which another person or group is persecuting the community or us or treating people in our community poorly. Rather than fighting back in a competitive way, we're to work toward the good: feeding and giving drinks to our enemies and making sure to stay firmly fixed in the good.

When looking at this passage through an ecological lens, in relation to participation in the body of Christ, the body includes one's enemies. Although the enemies are currently not engaging in actions that build up the body, if we do the same, we further harm the body. Instead of causing more harm, we're to do good, which will hopefully make them feel embarrassed enough to stop harming us and maybe even join in in a positive way.[96]

---

96 A note about Romans 13, which comes directly following: one could make a good case for this section of Romans 13:1–7 expanding to an even broader body, that of the body politic, the state. Paul is saying that to the extent that the governing authorities are "not a terror to good conduct but to bad," they are participating in the community of all life and should be followed—give respect and honor to whom it is due, to those who are helping to govern in positive ways. Then Romans

Therefore, Romans 12[97] moves us through different scales of bodies that we participate in: our own individual bodies, the body of Christ, which we can conceive at various scales, and those within or outside our congregation who are persecuting us but are still part of our broader body. Then there's the political body and the even larger body of everyone who is considered a "neighbor."

Each fractal is a recognizable representation of the pattern, but each one is different, and this creates space for huge amounts of diversity and for celebrating the differences we have while also recognizing one another as true and full expressions of the pattern. In ourselves, as individual organisms, we are whole: we contain the whole pattern. This speaks to the value and worth of each one. Each of us is special and important, each of us can experience and express God in our embodied existence, and each of us can participate fully as a member in the larger communities and bodies we are nested within.

I want to also suggest that our bodies as fractals at various scales are in the same pattern as God, perhaps not in a physical way, but God in some way has created in us a pattern of who God is. Genesis 1:26 says, "Let us make humans in our image." This infers 1) we're created to resemble God in some way, and 2) within God's self, God is multiple in some way: "Let's create humans in *our* image." We use the concept

---

13:8–10 sums up this section with, "love is the fulfilling of the law," and the injunction to love our neighbors as ourselves—and who is our neighbor? All the other bodies with whom we form the global household body. Cherice Bock, "Romans 12:17–13:10 & Quakers' Relation to the State," *Quaker Religious Thought* 116–117 (2011): 8–22.

97   And perhaps also Romans 13; see previous footnote.

of the Trinity to help us have a metaphor for how God is multiple and one, for how Jesus could be part of God and fully God and also not the fullness of God. While Friends do not generally spend a lot of time worrying which part of God does what, many Friends will still be familiar with the traditional terms for these parts of God, either Father, Son, and Holy Spirit; or Creator, Redeemer, and Sustainer.

The term "economy of the Trinity" is used to talk about the role and work done by different persons of the Godhead as God interacts with creation. If you'll recall, the Greek word *oikos* means house or household, and economy is from that root word, plus the word for law (*nomos*). So, economy has to do with establishing and carrying out the law of the household—basically, making sure the household community runs as it should. In the economy of the Trinity, each Person of the Godhead is doing a particular type of work to ensure that the global household is running smoothly.[98]

In the Eastern Orthodox tradition, the Persons of the Trinity are seen in dynamic relationship that is co-equal, and although they're each doing work, they're also working together, enacting love and care within themself, and that relationality reaches out to the rest of creation. There's a great word for this: *perichoresis*, the Divine dance. The Persons of the Trinity are engaged in this Divine dance, weaving in and out, aware of each other's movement, participating in meeting and anticipating one another's needs, and inviting us

98   Ioanna Sahinidou, "Christ: Oikos of the Cosmos: Panentheism," *The Ecumenical Review* 70, no. 4 (2018): 637–650, DOI:10.1111/erev.12390.

into the dance with them.[99] Within God's self, they are a relational being. They are a body after which we are patterned, and they enact the work of bringing life to the *oikumene* (global household). We sort of talked about the different Persons of the Trinity this week. (I accidentally formed a section around each of the Persons, really—section 2 is about the Incarnate One, section 3 focuses on the Creator, and section 4 highlights the Spirit.) We see them at work in the global household, the body of our planet.

Ecotheologian Sallie McFague calls the Earth the body of God because creation is the way we have to encounter God. We only exist in this lifetime as embodied beings, and we encounter God through our senses, including our spiritual senses, which are part of our embodied selves.[100] Many call this panentheism, stating that God is *in* all things, infusing them with God's presence.[101]

We talked about God as Light and Breath or Air and how God became incarnate and walked around in a human body, going camping with us. I also mentioned the Augustine quote about nature as the first book and the Bible as the second

---

99   For a helpful overview of the origins of many of these ideas related to the social Trinity, perichoresis, and ecotheology, see: Brian J. Lee, *Celebrating God's Cosmic Perichoresis: the eschatological panentheism of Jürgen Moltmann as a resource for an ecological Christian worship* (Eugene, OR: Pickwick Publications, 2011).

100 Sallie McFague, *The Body of God: An Ecological Theology* (Minneapolis, MN: Fortress Press, 1993).

101 E.g., Jürgen Moltmann, *God in Creation: A New Theology of Creation and the Spirit of God, The Gifford Lectures 1984–1985* (San Francisco: Harper & Row, 1985); Sahinidou, "Christ: Oikos of the Cosmos: Panentheism"; Kathryn E. Tanner, *Jesus, Humanity and the Trinity: A Brief Systematic Theology* (Minneapolis: Fortress Press, 2001).

book by which we can know God, and Augustine was not the only early church leader to express this. So, as we participate in our own embodied existence, as we offer our bodies before God as our spiritual act of worship, as we participate in the life of the church, the body of Christ, and as we participate in the community of all life, the *oikumene*, we encounter God. God is immanently relational within God's self and always inviting our participation in that relationship, always inviting us into the process of bringing creation to life. When we participate in the communities, ecosystems, and biosphere of this planet, when we make it so the flows of nutrients can best make their way through the veins of our watersheds, when we take care of the plants that cleanse the air and make possible healthy soil networks, we are participating in the *perichoresis*, the Divine dance to which God is inviting us in each moment.

Therefore, transitioning to the third aspect of this talk, I see our bodies as fractals of hope because, at each scale of our lives, we can participate in this Divine dance. We can take care of our own bodies and the communities of organisms that make their home in us. We can build up the body of Christ, which is our meeting communities, our yearly meetings, and our denomination. We can participate in the re-membering of our stories and histories as we work to heal our watersheds, and this means remembering that we're members of this broader community or body. We can learn from the people and other beings who share the space about how they participate in the Divine dance.

Finally, seeing ourselves as members of fractal-like bodies at each scale can help us imagine how to embody hope as Friends. Thinking of bodies as fractals feels hopeful to me because I can participate in the work being done at all scales, but I can see clearly that not all the work is mine. I can contribute my body—I can offer my body as a living sacrifice, and that contributes to the work of all the bodies I'm a part of on a larger scale. All the tiny organisms within my own body-community are then placed in the space of participating in the co-creating Divine dance. We are being patterns and examples, as George Fox suggested.[102] He said that being patterns and examples with our lives would help us walk cheerfully over the earth, answering that of God in everyone. When we live out the *perichoresis* by letting our lives preach, we open up space where we can recognize God at work in others, and they can recognize the same pattern in our embodied work.

Doing the work we are called to do as a communal body also feels hopeful when we think of that body as a fractal: we can't do the big work alone. We can each do our part and be faithful, but we need one another to also contribute in order to enact faithfulness on a larger scale. In ecology, the community is more than the sum of its parts: when all members of a community are present and able to perform their particular niche, they can flourish more than if they were separated and doing the same work without interaction. So it is with us. When we come together in all of our rich diversity, we are more than the sum of our individual parts; we are a collective body, able to function as an organism on a completely different scale.

A community at this scale has a different kind of lifespan,

---

102   George Fox in a letter from Launceston Gaol, 1656. Fox, *Journal*, 263.

too, so if we think of ourselves as cells within our global body, we can see that the body will go on long after us. We only need to do the work of our time. When we see our denomination as a body with a lifespan, we can contribute our work to the ongoing sustenance of that body while it needs to continue living, and we can participate in its death when it is time, as it goes back into the soil to become nutrients for the upwelling of new life.

I think one of the other ways that seeing ourselves as embodied fractals at different scales is hopeful is that we belong to one another: we are part of one organism. We can more clearly see that our own good is intimately tied to that of others. While there is definitely an element of competition for resources in the natural world, scientists are recognizing that a more accurate description of how species evolve is through symbiotic evolution: we learn how to work together to make sure everyone's needs are met.[103] Species that are good at working with other species are more likely to thrive. This sounds quite a bit like Paul's instructions in Romans 12, to work together, be hospitable, focus on love of neighbor, and care for enemies so that the body as a whole continues to thrive.

In many ways, humanity is excellent at symbiotic evolution: we have learned to cultivate species and spaces to benefit ourselves and our favorite other species so that we have a very cozy symbiotic relationship with them. But we have also tried to dominate by getting rid of species we don't like, such

---

103   The original article in this field of endosymbiotic theory
      is: Lynn Sagan, "On the origin of mitosing cells," *Journal
      of Theoretical Biology* 14, no. 3 (1967): 225–274, DOI:
      10.1016/0022-5193(67)90079-3.

as "pests" that eat our favorite crops—but we don't pause to find out what else they do in the ecosystem that provides our life support. When we are in a competitive mindset, we have to always be afraid there won't be enough: we're trying to manipulate the body to serve our own needs, and we have to watch out for all the other bodies that are trying to get their piece of the pie.

But in a perspective where we see ourselves as part of the larger body, we don't have to be afraid. We can release our fear because we know that the body is set up to take care of its parts. We can do our part to ensure its proper functioning, and we can trust there will be enough. This goes for our relationships with the land and other creatures, and it also goes for our relationship with other people and people groups. This can aid us as we try to shift our perspective from white supremacy and colonialism toward healing and seeing ourselves as participants in the community of all life.

This brings us back to the question that I posed in section 1: Does Quakerism need to continue? If so, what would faithfulness look like for us? I think the most important things we can work on are becoming a true community, a true body. A true body takes care of all its parts, making sure that each gets the nutrients it needs. The work that we're talking about is a radical reorientation of our understanding from seeing ourselves as individuals only to seeing ourselves as a part of a whole. I'm valuable and whole myself, and also, when I do the work of offering my body as a living sacrifice, I get to participate in the broader work. It can be scary to shift to this communal perspective because it takes so much trust, and we are incredibly vulnerable if we try to do it alone.

As we talked about in section 4, this work changes our perspective on property and economy, as well as our social and spiritual lives. Economy is the work of implementing the laws and ways of the household, of helping the household to function and flourish. Economy is participating in the Divine life through our own embodied existence; it's about relationship and care; it's about tending to our place and our responsibility as an act of care for all the others in our global body. Through our communal body, the *shalom* community can come into existence as we practice rhythms of the Spirit's breath and Sabbath rest. In order to break out of the economic systems in which we are currently bound, we need each other intensely because this is challenging and counter-cultural work—but it's the way our global body is set up to function.

If our bodies are fractals of hope, we can begin this work in our own bodies, breaking down our assumptions and norms about our economic and ecological relationships, and hopefully, this will have an impact on the bodies we're a part of at all scales. As larger-scale bodies do something similar, we can have an even broader impact. In these ways, our small, individual actions have a ripple effect as we transcend all the scales and layers of bodies of different sizes and participate in the Divine dance. Friends, if we are to continue into the Eco-Reformation, it requires us to think of ourselves and act like a body that values each one and that connects us directly to the body of God. I'll leave you with this query: In what ways are we as Friends particularly called to express our embodiment of the *perichoresis*, the Divine dance?

Index

K

L

M

N

O

P

9 781594 980343